Revolutions and Revolutionaries

Socialist History 22

Rivers Oram Press
London, Sydney and Chicago

Editorial Team
Kevin Morgan
Stephen Woodhams
Willie Thompson
Mike Waite
David Parker
David Morgan
Heather Williams
Julie Johnson

Editorial Advisors
Noreen Branson
Eric Hobsbawm
David Howell
Monty Johnstone
Victor Kiernan
David Marquand
Ben Pimlott
Pat Thane

All editorial enquiries to Kevin Morgan, Department of Government, University of Manchester M13 9PL or Kevin.Morgan@man.ac.uk. Reviews enquiries to Stephen Woodhams at SWood18045@aol.com

Published in 2002
by Rivers Oram Press, an imprint of Rivers Oram Publishers Ltd
144 Hemingford Road, London N1 1DE

Distributed in the USA by
Independent Publishers Group, Franklin Street, Chicago IL 60610
Distributed in Australia and New Zealand by
UNIReps, University of New South Wales, Sydney, NSW 2052

Set in Garamond by NJ Design Associates
and printed in Great Britain by T.J. International Ltd, Padstow

This edition copyright © 2002 Socialist History Society
The articles are copyright © 2002 Edward Acton, Allison Drew, Monty Johnstone, Boris Kagarlitsky, Francis King, John Newsinger, Hillel Ticktin

No part of this journal may be produced in any form, except for the quotation of brief passages in criticism, without the written permission of the publishers
The right of the contributors to be identified as the authors has been asserted by them in accordance with the Copyright, Designs and Patents Act 1988

British Library Cataloguing in Publication Data
A catalogue record for this publication is available from the British Library
ISBN 1 85489 150 2(hb)
ISBN 1 85489 151 0 (pb)
ISSN 0969 4331

Contents

Notes on Contributors   v

Editorial   vi

Irish Labour in a Time of Revolution   1
John Newsinger

Prisoner Number 3566   32
An interview with Joseph Leon Glazer
Allison Drew

The Historical Significance of the Russian Revolution   56
A roundtable discussion
Edward Acton, Monty Johnstone, Boris Kagarlitsky,
Francis King and Hillel Ticktin

Reviews   82

Books to be remembered (5):
John Peet, *The Long Engagement: Memoirs of a Cold War legend*   82
(John Saville)

Richard Sakwa, *Postcommunism* (Shivdeep Singh Grewal)   85

M. J. Turner, *British Politics in the Age of Reform* (John Callow)   89

Nigel Copsey, *Anti-Fascism in Britain* and Dave Renton,   91
Fascism, Anti-Fascism and Britain in the 1940s (Tobias Abse)

Janet Todd, *The Secret Life of Aphra Behn* (Peter Turner)   94

David Childs, *The Two Red Flags. European social democracy and Soviet communism since 1945* (Richard Cross) **98**

John Newsinger, *Orwell's Politics* (Rodney Barker) **100**

Susan Weissman, *Victor Serge: The course is set on hope* (Mike Waite) **102**

Vida Henning, *Woman in a Shabby Brown Coat* (Laurie Green) **105**

Diana Anhalt, *A Gathering of Fugitives. American political expatriates in Mexico 1948–1965* (Steve Parsons) **107**

Griselda Carr, *Pit Women. Coal communities in Northern England in the early twentieth century* (Meg Allen) **111**

Paul Allender, *What's Wrong with Labour? A critical history of the Labour Party in the twentieth century* (David Rubinstein) **113**

Paul Laity (ed.), *Left Book Club Anthology* (Andy Croft) **115**

Notes on Contributors

John Newsinger teaches at Bath Spa University College and is the author of *Fenianism in Mid-Victorian Britain* (1994) and *Orwell's Politics* (paperback edn, 2001).

Allison Drew teaches politics at the University of York. Her most recent book is *Discordant Comrades. Identities and Loyalties on the South African Left* (2000). She is currently working on a comparative study of the communist parties in the settler societies of South Africa and Algeria.

Edward Acton is professor of modern European history at the University of East Anglia. He is the author of *Rethinking the Russian Revolution* (1990) and co-editor of *Critical Companion to the Russian Revolution* (1997).

Boris Kagarlitsky is a sociologist based in Moscow. He is director of the Globalisation Institute in Moscow and editor of the political section of the weekly *Novaya Gazeta*. His most recent book in English is *Russia under Yeltsin and Putin*.

Francis King is a part-time lecturer and researcher on Soviet history at the University of East Anglia, a freelance translator, and treasurer of the Socialist History Society.

Monty Johnstone was for many years a member of the CPGB Theory and Ideology Committee and has written widely on Soviet history, Marxism and the international communist movement.

Hillel Ticktin is professor of Marxist studies at the Centre for Socialist Theory and Movements, Glasgow University. He has written extensively on the Soviet Union and after, and is editor of *Critique, Journal of Socialist Theory*.

Editorial

The main articles in this issue of *Socialist History* are concerned with international themes—Ireland, South Africa and Russia—in the first half of the last century. John Newsinger reassesses the history of the Irish labour movement at a pivotal phase in its history—the years immediately preceding and following the First World War. Labour struggles have tended to be neglected, or subsumed into the story of the national struggle and the self-sacrificial heroism of the Easter Rising of 1916. This has led to much greater stress on the role of James Connolly, and a relative neglect of the contribution of Jim Larkin and the syndicalist current in Irish labour history. In his article John Newsinger has attempted to redress the balance, as well as to explore the complex interrelationship between class politics, republicanism and Catholicism in the southern Irish labour movement.

Allison Drew sets the scene for a remarkable human document—an interview with the son of the only unofficial pre-war political emigrant from South Africa to the USSR. Joseph Glazer was the son of Henry Glazer, one of the earliest members of the Communist Party of South Africa. Henry Glazer emigrated with his son to the USSR in the early 1930s, enthusiastic and optimistic about being able to contribute to the construction of socialism. The fates of both father and son were tragic. Henry Glazer disappeared into the gulag system within a few years, never to be seen again. His son, Joseph Glazer, was arrested in 1949, as a new wave of xenophobia, this time with strongly anti-semitic undercurrents, began to engulf the Soviet Union. Joseph survived to be released in 1957, and continues to live in Russia.

The third feature is in the nature of an experiment: a roundtable discussion on the historical significance of the Russian Revolution, conducted, not in person like our previous roundtable on the future of history (*Socialist History* 14), but by e-mail. There were several advantages in having the discussion by e-mail, foremost of which was the ability to involve participants in different cities and even countries over an extended period, giving them the opportunity to make more considered responses to each other's views. On this occasion, five people took part, from Britain and Russia, and the discussion ranged widely over many of the points of dispute on the history of the revolution and its significance. Predictably enough, no consensus was reached on this still most controversial of topics.

We are sorry to learn that in Duncan Thompson's article 'Pessimism of the intellect' (*Socialist History* 20), certain errors have occurred during copy-editing. Page 21, line 3, states: 'After [E.P.] Thompson relinquished control, the *New Left Review*'s principal preoccupations continued to be popular culture...' Thompson did not in fact ever 'control' the *NLR*, and the intended sense of the original article was that it was he and the first New Left, not the *NLR*, whose preoccupations continued to be popular culture and the recovery of working-class history 'from below'. Page 24, line 31 should have indicated that Anthony Barnett, Fred Halliday, Alexander Cockburn, Gareth Stedman Jones and Peter Wollen from the *NLR* were involved with the weekly newspaper *Seven Days*. Our apologies to readers and to Duncan Thompson.

JOIN THE SOCIALIST HISTORY SOCIETY

Membership entitles you to attend all the Society's events, to receive two numbers of Socialist History per year plus two pamphlets, and to participate in its decision making.

Subscription rates are:

UK individual full £18.00 (£22.50 overseas);
UK individual concessionary £12.00 (£17.00 overseas);
£20.00 labour movement organisations

Kevin Morgan
Department of Government
University of Manchester
Manchester M13 9PL

e-mail: Kevin.Morgan@man.ac.uk

Irish Labour in a Time of Revolution

John Newsinger

The comparative neglect of Irish labour history in international labour history studies is quite clearly demonstrated in three very different collections of essays: Marcel van der Linden and Wayne Thorpe's *Revolutionary Syndicalism. An international perspective*, Chris Wrigley's *Challenges of Labour. Central and Western Europe, 1917–1920*, and Sam Davies and others' *Dock Workers*, published as recently as 2000.[1] The van der Linden and Thorpe collection has useful chapters on syndicalism in France, Holland, Germany, Sweden, Britain, Spain, Portugal, Italy, Argentina, Mexico, Canada and the United States, but no chapter on Ireland. The rise of the Irish Transport and General Workers' Union (ITGWU) under the leadership of Big Jim Larkin, the syndicalist writings of Jim Connolly, and the attempt to build the One Big Union in a period of revolution and civil war are absent. It is not a case of the work not having been done: Connolly is almost certainly the most written about syndicalist propagandist and theorist there has been, the ITGWU has an excellent official history by the late C. Desmond Greaves, a lifelong communist and one of the founders of modern Irish labour history, and the postwar syndicalist explosion has been the subject of an excellent path-breaking study by Emmet O'Connor.[2] Similarly, Chris Wrigley's collection examines the revolutionary ferment that momentarily affected Germany, Hungary, Austria, Italy, France and Britain, in particular Scotland, but once again there is no chapter on the Irish experience. The 1916 Easter Rising, the 1918 general strike against conscription, the 1919 Belfast engineering strike and the sectarian shipyard expulsions the following year, the great syndicalist explosion throughout the south of Ireland, that movement's eventual defeat, the failure of Irish communism, the impact of partition, and underlying all these developments, the complex dialectic of class consciousness and national revolution are surely of more than parochial importance. Once again, considerable work has been done, more remains to be done, but it is all marginal to international labour history. And the same holds true for Sam Davies and others' magnificent two-volume collection, *Dock Workers*. This contains twenty-two port studies that range from Shanghai to Hull, from Hamburg to Fremantle, from Liverpool to New York, from Bombay to Mombassa, from Turku to San Francisco, but there is no account of Dublin or the struggles of the Dublin dockers. Indeed, more generally, a good case can be made that we know more about Irish dockers in London, New York and Glasgow than about those in Dublin. This neglect is mistaken. The historical experience of the Irish working class, especially during the Great Labour Unrest, the War of Independence and the civil war that followed, deserves greater attention and wider notice than it has so far received outside of Ireland.

One point worth making here is that discussion will focus on the Catholic and Nationalist labour movement in the south of the country.

The rise of the ITGWU

The rise of the ITGWU in the years before the outbreak of the First World War was part of the great labour unrest that characterized British industrial relations in this period.[3] The new union organised the unskilled workers of Dublin and other Irish towns, arguably succeeding in making Dublin one of the best-organised cities in Europe, if not the world. Larkin and his lieutenants even succeeded in extending the benefits of trade union organisation to the downtrodden farm labourers of County Dublin. This was a tremendous achievement, especially considering the conditions that obtained in Catholic Ireland. Dublin itself was a commercial and trading rather than an industrial centre with a large unskilled working class that endured some of the worst social conditions in Western Europe. In 1911, there were only 1,148 engineering workers in Dublin, but 17,262 general labourers, men and women whose precarious employment made it very difficult for them to organise. Indeed, all previous efforts had ended in failure. Wages were low and living conditions were appalling: over 20,000 families, fully one third of the total, were living in one room, far worse conditions than existed in Belfast, Liverpool, Manchester or Glasgow.[4] According to one commentator, the Gothic pinnacles of St. Patrick's Cathedral looked down directly on a slum district 'where the degradation of human kind is carried to a point of abjectness beyond that reached in any city of the Western world, save perhaps Naples'.[5] Nevertheless, the ITGWU was to succeed where others had failed.

How was this achieved? By militancy, solidarity and the sympathetic strike. For the ITGWU, working class solidarity was the key to successfully organising the unskilled workforce. This was the union's central ethic around which all else revolved. Any section or group of workers in dispute could rely on the active support of the rest of the union membership, support not just in terms of financial assistance but also of industrial action. Picket lines were scrupulously respected and 'tainted' goods were never touched. The 'sympathetic strike' was the crucial instrument for breaking employer resistance, so that no group of workers went down to defeat in isolation. This was particularly important in circumstances of a surplus of unskilled labour where employers often broke strikes by the wholesale replacement of the strikers with strikebreakers. Now, the entire working class was to be enrolled in One Big Union that would confront the employing class as a united army that could no longer be divided and ruled. As the union newspaper, the Irish Worker, put it: 'Let the workers stand firmly together, shoulder-to-shoulder, just as the masters do. Let the demand come from all—one union for all workers, and the capitalist class could not resist…' Strikes were conducted aggressively so as to isolate the employer and discourage scabbing while strikers were sustained by the solidarity of other union members. A good example of this process at work is provided by the account of a lockout of women workers at the Savoy Confectionery Company that appeared in the pages of the *Irish Worker* in the summer of 1913. On 5 July, the newspaper reported that the Company had been unable to hire a van driver from the Labour Exchange because of the dispute, that the city's carters 'pass the Savoy as though it were a place in which the plague was raging', that packages put on the trams for collection 'were kicked off into the street', and that the union was 'going to deal' with 'Waytes, the scab motor firm' that was supplying the Company with taxis. Firms that had dealings with the Savoy company were warned off in the pages of the *Irish Worker* and on one occasion it printed the names and addresses of the scabs McMurty had hired to try and break the union.[6] These challenging tactics were an aspect of what was an unprecedented revolt of the unskilled working class, and the man who became the embodiment of that revolt was Big Jim Larkin.[7]

Larkin first achieved prominence with his part in the 1907 transport strike in Belfast and then the following year successfully organised the dockers and carters in Dublin.[8] By the end of 1908, he had established the British National Union of Dock Labourers in every port in Ireland, but his militant methods alarmed the union leadership and, in particular, its general secretary, James Sexton, who already regarded Larkin as a rival. On 8 December 1908, Larkin was suspended from his post. Later that month, on the 28th, he launched a breakaway union committed to organising all categories of unskilled workers, the Irish Transport and General Workers' Union. He took with him the great bulk of the NUDL's Irish membership, outside of Belfast.[9] To begin with, union membership was denied to women workers, but in September 1911 a sister organisation, the Irish Women Workers Union was established.[10] One often neglected point worth making here is that the Irish were not alone in their dissatisfaction with the NUDL leadership: in July 1911 Glasgow dockers broke away to form the Scottish Union of Dock Labourers with Sexton's treatment of Larkin a significant factor.[11]

Attempts were made to destroy the ITGWU in much the same way as previous attempts at organising unskilled workers had been destroyed, but the rising tide of industrial unrest that gripped both Britain and Ireland sustained the new union. The year 1911 was decisive in this regard, as membership grew from a precarious 5000 to some 18,000. That same year, on 27 May, Larkin launched the union newspaper, the *Irish Worker* that was to rally the working class and pour scorn and abuse on its opponents. The newspaper was to achieve a weekly sale of around 20,000 copies.[12]

Larkin's approach to trade union organisation was evangelical. He came not just to secure union recognition and collective agreement, but to raise the working class up and to create a new world. Lord Askwith recalled one Dublin employer remarking on the difficulty of dealing with Larkin: 'You can't argue with the prophet Isaiah'; and this, Askwith acknowledged, was 'not an inapt description of a man who came to believe he had a mission on earth'.[13] Larkin's great strength was his ability to articulate the anger and rage, the hopes and longings, of the Dublin working class. According to Constance Markiewicz, it seemed, when she heard him address the crowds, as if 'his personality caught up, assimilated and threw back to the vast crowd that surrounded him every emotion that swayed them, every pain and joy that they had ever felt made articulated and sanctified'.[14]

Larkin's was an insurgent trade unionism that mobilised men and women who had hitherto been completely at the mercy of their employers. To force those employers to recognise and negotiate agreements with a militant trade union that made the sympathetic strike and the doctrine of tainted goods the cornerstones of its organising strategy was an overturning of the accepted order of things. The ITGWU gave hope and self-confidence to working people who had previously had to be content with survival on their employers' terms. It gave organised form and inspiring voice to a determination to shift the balance of class forces in Irish society in favour of the working class and offered the prospect of a new world where labour ruled. Larkin proclaimed in the *Irish Worker* that 'a newer type of man and woman is being formed amongst the working class; a new era opens out to us…the end being a mutual Commonwealth built on service, a broadening out of the perspective of life, a fuller and more complete life, the obliterating of class rule and distinction of caste—a day when work, useful and beautiful, will be the test…'[15] This challenging of the prerogatives of the Dublin employers was something more than routine trade unionism founded on compromise and collaboration. Certainly, this was what well-informed contemporaries believed. According to Arnold Wright, putting the employers' view, Larkins 'movement stands quite outside the ordinary category of labour disturbances'. It was 'a revolutionary rising', the promoters of which intended 'the destruction of society quite as much as the betterment of the wage conditions of the workers'.[16] While, Lord Askwith, a man with immense experience of industrial conflict, observed that: 'If the disputes in the ports and inland cities of Great Britain had been chiefly based upon economic causes, the serious riots in Dublin, although founded upon poverty, low wages and bad conditions, included determination to establish the transport workers' union as the "one big union" in Ireland and put into practice the doctrines of syndicalism…The influences of "ca'canny" propaganda, the overthrow of Capitalism and revolution against existing authority were all present'.[17] What we are confronted with has been best described by Bob Holton as 'proto-syndicalism', something that was less than social revolutionary consciousness, but more than trade union consciousness. It contained within it the potential to develop into a full-blooded challenge to the existing social and economic order rather than indicating any acceptance of it.[18] In the Irish context, this 'proto-syndicalism' was known to friends and enemies alike as 'Larkinism'.

Two other important aspects of the ITGWU's ideology require consideration here: Nationalism and Catholicism. From its very inception, the union was staunchly nationalist, rejecting Home Rule as a betrayal and embracing instead separatism and republicanism. This commitment was, it must be insisted, not the work of Jim Connolly, but rather reflected the long-established republican traditions of at least a section of the Dublin working class, a tradition that embraced the United Irishmen of the 1790s, the Confederate clubs of 1848, the Fenians of the 1860s, and the Fenian rally to Parnell of 1890–91.[19] The *Irish Worker* revived and gave powerful voice to that tradition at a time when the surviving republican organisation, the secret Irish Republican Brotherhood (IRB), had only some 1200–1500 mainly middle-class members.[20] In the newspaper's first issue, Larkin proclaimed that 'We owe no allegiance to any other nation nor the king, governors, or representatives of any other nation'. Such people were 'interlopers and trespassers on this our land'. But, the *Irish Worker* was not out just for 'National Freedom', but for 'Individual Freedom', that is freedom from 'economic or wage slavery'.[21] On 15 July 1911, on the occasion of King

George V's visit to Dublin, the *Irish Worker* celebrated the thousand people who visited Wolfe Tone's grave rather than bow down to 'the Pirate Empire'. It proclaimed that while there 'is even one of our people ill-clad or ill-treated, we will join in no display of hypocritical loyalty'. The newspaper stated that its great ambition was 'to nationalise the wealth and production of the country', but that to accomplish this 'we must first nationalise the people, then the Government'.[22]

The republican stance taken by the ITGWU at this time could not be clearer. Working-class republicanism was an essential component of the phenomenon of Larkinism. It was taken up quite independently of Jim Connolly, reflecting the beliefs and commitments of the union leadership and of the active core of its membership. Many accounts of the period, in particular the various biographical studies of Connolly, discuss developments as if Connolly was almost the lone advocate of republicanism within the labour movement. This was not the case. A better way to conceptualise Connolly's position is to regard him as trying to develop a Marxist theorisation for working-class republicanism, as trying to give Marxist expression to an already existing working-class tradition. His celebrated *Labour in Irish History* was very much such an exercise. Where Larkin and Connolly were to disagree was over the extent to which they were prepared to ally with the middle class republicans. Under Larkin, the *Irish Worker* remained fiercely critical of middle class republicanism and of the Irish volunteers (Sean O'Casey was the main spokesperson for this view), while under Connolly it was to move towards an accommodation with them that was to culminate in the Easter Rising.[23]

More remarkable than the ITGWU's republicanism, however, was its Catholicism. Larkin himself, together with the great majority of the union's membership were devout Catholics, living and working in a country where the Catholic Church had considerable popular support and great influence. Even Connolly felt obliged to pose as a Catholic.[24] This was and still is often difficult for non-Catholic socialists unfamiliar with the Irish situation to come to terms with.

Larkin's Catholicism did not stop Catholic priests attacking the ITGWU or its other enemies using the press to denounce it for atheism, for supporting divorce and birth control, and for being the work of the Anti-Christ. The *Irish Worker* responded to these attacks vigorously. In the early weeks of the great Dublin lockout, Larkin, a teetotaler, replied to an attack on the union by a Father Condon. He pointed out that the 'Reverend Father' had forgot to mention that he was a shareholder in a firm affected by the dispute, the non-union Guinness brewery, 'taking profits from a trade of which one cannot find words adequate to describe the horrors caused by its continuance'. And, he went on, what about 'the seventy odd priests who are shareholders in the Dublin United Tramway Company and who are responsible along with that other pillar of the Church, William "Murder" Murphy for the terrible bloodshed and tragedy of death'. Had Father Condon no criticism of these clergy whose self-interest actually required the defeat of the union? 'Thank God', he concluded, 'there are others who dignify the high and holy calling, who instead of attacking the working class, sympathise with their efforts'.[25] Such priests were few and far between, but Larkin and his comrades nevertheless regarded them as a vindication of their continued faith.

Despite this, the Catholic Church stood with the employers in the Dublin Lockout. Its most dramatic intervention occurred at the end of October 1913 when the union attempted to send the children of strikers on holiday with sympathisers in Britain. While there was certainly some sincere fear of proselytism (although too many historians have accepted this at face value), the clerical efforts to thwart the scheme were primarily motivated by a desire to attack the Larkinites, to combat the socialist contagion they saw infecting the poor. Middle class priests led large aggressive crowds of hymn-singing supporters to physically seize hold of children and prevent them leaving the city. While there was some concern that the energetic nature of the clerical response to the scheme might alienate working-class Catholics from the Church, what is remarkable is that neither the leadership nor the rank and file of the ITGWU embraced the sort of virulent anti-clericalism that was very much a feature of the labour movements in other European countries where there was a strong Catholic Church. One thing was clear, however: while the Dublin clergy were zealous to prevent children's souls being put at risk, they completely failed in their duty to look after their bodies through the provision of charitable relief.

The Dublin Lockout

The Dublin Lockout that began in August 1913 inflicted a crushing defeat on the ITGWU that ended the Larkinite advance. Larkin's efforts to secure union recognition from William Murphy's Tramway Company, something that seemed well within the union's capabilities, came up against first the power of the state and then a counter-attack by the Dublin Employers' Association.[26] On 26 August, the union called its members on the trams out on strike in retaliation against the victimisation of a growing number of union members. Even though many men remained at work, there could be little doubt that aggressive picketing would soon bring them out and close the trams down. This was not to be. Murphy had the full support of the authorities in this confrontation, the union leadership was arrested for seditious libel and conspiracy, and the police were turned loose to drive the crowds of union pickets off the streets and ensure that a tram service of some kind was maintained. Over the weekend of 30–31 August, in fierce clashes the police beat to death two union members, injured hundreds more and arrested over 200 people. The police invaded tenements, smashing furniture and assaulting and intimidating women and children. This display of state repression rallied the rest of the Dublin employers to Murphy's side and they declared a general lockout against the ITGWU. Employment was refused to all those who refused to sign a 'document' forswearing the union. Eventually nearly 25,000 workers employed by over 400 employers were to be either locked out or were on strike. The struggle was to continue until in mid-January 1914 the union ordered its members to return to work on whatever terms they could get. Some 5,000 workers were still locked out in mid-February and the women of Jacob's biscuits, a Larkinite stronghold, did not go back until the middle of March. Many, of course, were never allowed back and found themselves blacklisted and unemployed instead. Union membership plummeted and it seemed that the Larkinite advance had been decisively rolled back. The struggle has been marvellously chronicled by Pádraig Yeates in his *Lockout Dublin 1913* published in 2000.[27]

Why did the ITGWU lose? The courage, endurance and loyalty of the union's membership proved unable to overcome the united determination of the Dublin employers backed up by the police, the clergy, the judiciary (over 400 strikers were imprisoned during the lockout) and the press. The employers even went so far as to covertly finance two scab labour newspapers, *The Liberator* and *The Toiler*, that week after week accused Larkin of atheism, corruption, cowardice, treachery, Protestantism, Mormonism, of being in the pay of the English, and of being the son of Carey the Informer.[28] In the end, however, three factors can be identified as being decisive. First, the general nature of the lockout made it impossible for the union to isolate any individual employer who would then have had to withstand the whole resources of the union. This had forced many employers to concede recognition, but now they rallied to Murphy. Second, once effective picketing was stopped by police action and scabs were brought in, the union was put on the defensive. Without recourse to sympathetic strikes, the blacking of tainted goods or aggressive pickets, the union found itself engaged in a war of attrition that the employers showed every intention of continuing until the workers were starved back to work. The third factor was the failure of solidarity action in Britain.

Larkin quite correctly realised that the only way to avoid defeat was to secure solidarity action from the British labour movement, to secure the blacking of goods from Dublin that were being produced and transported by scab labour. His campaign to secure solidarity action in Britain has been criticised by many historians as counter-productive, as unnecessarily alienating British trade union leaders and thereby actually weakening support for the Dublin workers.[29] This view misunderstands the nature of the situation that confronted Larkin. There was no possibility of a compromise settlement of the dispute. Whereas the ITGWU accepted efforts at mediation, the employers refused. They were out to destroy Larkin's union. In these circumstances, while the TUC's financial aid was vital in enabling the union to continue the fight, it was never going to win it. Only the blacking of Dublin traffic in Britain could have achieved that. Prospects of securing solidarity action from the official leadership of the British trade union movement were realistically nil. But this was a period of rank and file insurgency, of unofficial strikes. What Larkin called for on his 'fiery cross' crusade was rank and file action to black Dublin traffic in the hope and expectation that this would pressure the official leadership into taking action. He was addressing a definite constituency of trade union militants and political activists who distrusted their own leaders and looked to Larkin as the spokesperson for an uncompromising insurgent movement of revolt.[30] Larkin's mistake lay not in conducting his campaign for solidarity, but rather in the extent to which he put his faith in various leftwing trade union leaders such as Ben Tillett. Certainly, Larkin's campaign had an effect, forcing the first ever TUC special conference to discuss the situation in Dublin on 9 December, but on the day it was dominated by full-time officials. As R. M. Fox has pointed out, while ostensibly it was called 'to decide what was to be done about Dublin', in reality 'it was to decide what was to be done about Larkin'.[31] The conference censured Larkin for his attacks on British trade union leaders and overwhelmingly rejected the call for solidarity action. After this, the ITGWU's defeat was certain. Only solidarity action could have saved Larkin's union and this was refused. In Jim Connolly's embittered words: 'We asked for the isolation of the capitalists of Dublin, and for answer the leaders of the British labour movement proceeded calmly to isolate the working class of Dublin'. Instead of 'the sacramental wafer of brotherhood and common sacrifice' (an interesting choice of phrase), the workers of Dublin had to 'eat the dust of defeat and betrayal'.[32]

There is one last point worth making with regard to the rise of the ITGWU and the Dublin Lockout: the nature of the relationship between Larkin and Connolly. Connolly has come to completely dominate the historiography of the period. Since the early 1920s he has been the subject of at least fifteen book-length studies, starting with Desmond Ryan's *James Connolly* published in 1924 and continuing most recently with Kieran Allen's *The Politics of James Connolly* published in 1990 and W. K. Anderson's *James Connolly and the Irish Left* published in 1994.[33] Larkin, on the other hand, has been the subject of only four book-length studies, one by R. M. Fox, published in 1957, another, the standard biography, by Emmet Larkin published in 1968, a family history by Larkin's grandson that was published in 1995, and most recently the celebratory volume edited by Donal Nevin in 1998.[34] This amounts to a serious distortion of the relative importance of the two men, a distortion that derives not from Connolly's work as a trade union leader, as a socialist politician or even as a Marxist theoretician, but from his participation in the Easter Rising that gave him an inflated posthumous importance. This was reinforced by the conflict that was to break out within the Irish labour movement between Larkin and William O'Brien in the 1920s. O'Brien and his supporters denigrated Larkin's contribution to the labour movement and instead celebrated and exaggerated that of the by now safely dead Connolly.[35] This process is continued even in C. Desmond Greaves's otherwise outstanding official history of the ITGWU, where he does not miss any opportunity to diminish Larkin, to call into question his judgement and temperament, even to question his mental stability.[36] This will not do. As Sean O'Casey, a lifelong Larkinite, was to argue, somewhat poetically, in the *Irish Citizen* newspaper: 'The flame that burns in the heart of the Irish Labour Movement, whether we like it or not, was lit by Jim Larkin and lit by none other'.[37]

The Easter Rising

After the ITGWU's defeat in the Dublin Lockout, Larkin left for the United States at the end of October 1914 to try and raise funds for the bankrupt union. He was not to return until April 1923.[38] He somewhat reluctantly agreed to Jim Connolly replacing him as acting-General Secretary. While Connolly continued the process of trying to rebuild the union, his overriding concern increasingly became the need to stage an armed insurrection against the British. Connolly had always been concerned with the relationship between the struggle for socialism and the national struggle. He had argued on a number of occasions that only the working class would be able to liberate Ireland because only they could break the economic chains binding the country. In the process, the Irish working class would also free itself. Consequently, the working class had to assume the leadership in the national struggle. This was most emphatically not the position that he was to put into effect in the months leading up to the Easter Rising. Instead of the working class taking the lead in the national struggle, Connolly was to ally his tiny Citizen Army (less than 200 members) with the Fenian secret society, the Irish Republican Brotherhood (IRB) with the intention of staging a rising regardless of the prospects of success. As Richard English puts it, having 'argued strongly against republican all-class alliances', Connolly went on to play 'a leading role in a cross-class republican project'.[39] This was very much a response on his part to the ITGWU's defeat in the lockout, to the proposed partition of the country and to the failure of the international working class movement to oppose the World War.

The Rising was organised by the IRB's Military Council, a body whose members were motivated less by belief in military success than by the conviction that the very existence of a separate Irish nation was at stake because of the widespread Irish support for the British war effort. A blood sacrifice had to be made, in Connolly's words, to 'keep alive the soul of the nation'.[40] The chief advocate of this doctrine within the IRB was Padraic Pearse, but Connolly increasingly proclaimed it as well. In a celebrated article that appeared only weeks before the rising, he condemned the majority of the Irish working class for having sold their country, and warned: 'Without the slightest trace of irreverence but in all due humility and awe, we recognise that of us, as of mankind before Calvary, it may truly be said: "Without the shedding of Blood, there can be no Redemption"'.[41]

Connolly, a lifelong critic of physical force republicanism, was sworn into the IRB, co-opted onto its Military Council and appointed to the command of all the rebel forces in Dublin. Far from the working class taking over the leadership in the national struggle, Connolly led a tiny minority into an alliance with the republicans, on their terms. He was acting very much on his own behalf rather than as the leader or representative of the labour movement. He was the only member of the ITGWU's fourteen-man executive to take part in the rising and made no serious attempt to rally the union's rank and file membership, still recovering from the Great Lockout. In 1916, the union only had some 5,000 members. Connolly made no attempt to call a general strike in support of the rising; instead the union's membership remained, by and large, passive observers. One simple reason for this failure was that such a strike call would not have met with any success because, as the rebel leaders were well aware, there was no popular support for their adventure and, anyway, the unions were too weak. Indeed, in 1916 there were considerably more ITGWU members fighting with the British Army in France than took part in the Easter Rising.[42] A good case can be made that working-class participation in the events of Easter Week was largely confined to taking advantage of the withdrawal of the police to engage in widespread looting.[43] According to one account: 'for days to come all kinds of luxuries could be bought in Dublin slums for a trifle. You could have a silver fox fur for a shilling or two; a pair of hand-made boots for what you cared to give; and a gold watch for half a crown'. The post-Rising police raids in working-class districts were not in search of fleeing rebels, but searches for stolen property.[44]

One of the earliest critics of Connolly's stance in 1916 was Sean O'Casey, himself a former member of the IRB, now a staunch Larkinite who had for a while been secretary of the Citizen Army. He had not taken part in the rising but subsequently remained in touch with its leadership. In 1919, he published *The Story of the Irish Citizen Army* in which he accused Connolly of surrendering the political independence of the labour movement by making the Citizen Army 'the militant Left Wing of the Irish Volunteers'. He wrote of 'the almost revolutionary change that was manifesting itself in Connolly's nature' in the months before Easter Week, of how he seemed to regard the labour movement as a 'decrescent force' and that he had abandoned 'the narrow byway of Irish Socialism' for 'the broad and crowded highway of Irish Nationalism'. As far as O'Casey was concerned Connolly's political activities in the months before the rising 'proclaimed trumpet-tongued that the appeal of Caitlin Nih Ullachain—"if anyone would give me help, he must give me himself, he must give me all"—was in his ears a louder cry than the appeal of the Internationale'. He believed that the Irish working class had 'lost a leader'.[45] Other contemporaries on the left shared O'Casey's view. Louie Bennett believed that Connolly had seen 'a chance of grasping freedom for Ireland and from that moment Labour took second place in his thoughts'. He had, she believed, been 'feverishly infected by what we politely call war fever'.[46] Thomas Johnston, the editor of the Glasgow newspaper, *Forward*, that was banned in January 1916, later remembered how puzzled he had been that Connolly, 'a cool, level-headed analyst, precise, careful, and accustomed to weighing evidence and words…had ever come to be a leader in an armed rebellion against the British Government, when his Citizen Army insurgents could only muster 118 rifles'. None of Connolly's articles for *Forward* had 'ever given hint that he was developing into a military insurrectionist Sinn Feiner'.[47] Shortly before his execution, Connolly conceded the case to these critics when he told his daughter, Nora, that foreign socialists 'will never understand why I am here. They will all forget I am an Irishman'.[48]

This critical view was soon overwhelmed by what can be usefully described as the Connolly cult. Instead of his participation in the Easter

Rising being seen as an aberration from his socialist politics, it came to be seen as their culmination. This interpretation was to be given its most sophisticated expression by C. Desmond Greaves in his 1961 biography, *The Life and Times of James Connolly*. Here he argued that Connolly had developed his own version of the 'stages theory' whereby the national struggle had to be completed before the struggle for socialism could be undertaken. When he allied with the IRB in 1916, he was, according to Greaves, quite consciously engaged in trying to achieve national independence so as to be able to proceed to the next stage. Greaves actually quotes Connolly as referring to 'the first stage of freedom'. There is, however, no evidence that Connolly adhered to a stages theory and as John Hoffman has shown Greaves had in fact misquoted from an article that appeared in the *Workers' Republic* on 15 January 1916. What Connolly actually wrote referred not to the 'first stage' but to the very different 'first days of freedom'. Elsewhere Greaves argued that in a speech delivered to the Citizen Army only a short while before the rising, Connolly told them 'to hold on to your rifles, as those with whom we are fighting may stop before our goal is reached. We are out for economic as well as political liberty'. The trouble with this quotation, which is faithfully reproduced in a number of subsequent accounts, is that it has no reliable provenance and is contradicted by everything that we know for certain that Connolly did actually say and write.[49] The fact that Connolly never said that his participation in the Easter Rising was part of the struggle for socialism but did on numerous occasions say that it was to save or redeem the soul of the nation has led to some remarkable contortions on the part of upholders of the Greaves orthodoxy. Most recently W. K. Anderson has asserted that it is 'abundantly clear' that Connolly was fighting for socialism in 1916 and then actually goes on to say that some 'statement, perhaps even a proclamation of some kind stating clearly the goal of a Workers' Republic, would have been of immense assistance…' Indeed, it would.[50] There is also a quite incredible reluctance to admit that Connolly adopted a pro-German stance during the First World War. The evidence is incontrovertible but is simply ignored in favour of the quite unsubstantiated claim that he had the same position as Lenin.[51]

The Greaves orthodoxy has come under challenge from a number of historians. David Howell argued that Connolly made 'ideological compromises' in 1916, that he believed the circumstances of the time made it necessary for him to compromise aspects of his socialist politics.[52] More full-bloodedly, Austen Morgan argued that Connolly's alliance with the IRB involved him abandoning socialism and internationalism and instead embracing nationalism. He died a republican not a socialist martyr.[53] While both these interpretations are certainly more soundly based than the Greaves interpretation, they are still inadequate. More reliable is the argument that Connolly remained a socialist but that in the conditions of wartime Ireland he no longer believed his socialist politics of immediate relevance and so put them to one side. Instead, he came to the conclusion that the urgent question of the moment was to preserve Irish national identity from the danger of extinction and accordingly he embraced the doctrine of the blood sacrifice. This involved him in a hopeless republican putsch, cost him his life, and deprived the Irish working class of a much-needed leader.

One last point about Connolly: he provides further testimony to the strength of Catholicism within the Irish working class. While for most of his life he was an agnostic, he admitted that he 'posed' as a Catholic. To have done otherwise would have ended any chance he had of playing a leading role in the labour movement. Nevertheless, the evidence does suggest that before his execution he was reconciled with the Church. When he last saw his wife, a Protestant, shortly before his execution, he urged her to convert to Catholicism and she subsequently did.[54] Another instance of the devotion of the Citizen Army men is provided by Connolly's second-in-command, Michael Mallin, who before his execution wrote to his wife that 'Ireland will come out greater and grander but she must not forget she is Catholic, she must keep faith'. He urged that his son, Joseph become a priest, and his daughter, Una, a nun.[55] Constance Markiewicz, another leading member of the Citizen Army and a Protestant of sorts subsequently converted to Catholicism, inspired as she told her friend, Esther Roper, by the spiritual example of 'the simple and unlettered men of the Irish Citizen Army'.[56]

Labour and Sinn Féin

When the Irish Trade Union Congress met at Sligo on 7 August 1916 its chairman, Thomas Johnson, made clear to delegates that now was not the time to discuss 'the right or wrong, the wisdom or the folly, of the revolt'. He did nevertheless propose a minute's remembrance for Connolly and the other trade unionists who had died fighting against the British and also for Irishmen who had died fighting for the British in France and the Middle East. He made absolutely clear his own support for the Allied war effort. In this way, Congress with the acquiescence of the strong ITGWU delegation, quite deliberately refused to endorse the Easter Rising and similarly refused to oppose the war. Greaves cannot help but express his surprise at the failure of 'this crucial test': 'no voice was raised to avow Connolly's programme of revolutionary opposition to the war, not even that of William O'Brien'.[57]

This was partly to avoid precipitating a split with Protestant delegates from the North, partly to save the movement in the South from further British repression, but it also reflected the cautious moderation of the labour movement's leaders. As one historian has aptly observed, Johnson was much more the Fabian than he was the Fenian.[58]

The labour movement's leadership, dominated at this time by Johnson, William O'Brien and others, regarded the national struggle as something altogether separate from their principal task of building strong trade unions and establishing a credible Labour Party. Rather than the labour movement providing the leadership in the national struggle, or even entering into an alliance with middle class republicanism, they saw its role as ancillary, as one of providing limited support for those actually engaged in the struggle to achieve independence. Labour's struggles were separate and apart from the republican cause though on occasions the strength of the working class would be mobilised in its support. Arguably, this handed political leadership in Ireland over to the Sinn Féin alliance, a surrender from which the Irish labour movement has never really recovered. As one contemporary critic put it, 'the Labour Movement entered into the compact as a vassal rather than a co-partner'.[59] While subordination to Sinn Féin was to be the political stance taken up by the labour movement in this period, as far as the trade unions were concerned, the years after Easter Week were also a period of massive expansion, a period during which a wave of syndicalist agitation engulfed both rural and urban Ireland. The failure of the Johnson-O'Brien leadership to use this increasing industrial strength, to place themselves in the forefront of the national struggle is one of the great missed opportunities in modern European labour history.

The increasing strength of the labour movement was most clearly demonstrated with regard to the opposition to British plans to introduce conscription into Ireland. The worsening situation on the Western Front forced the British to prepare for this regardless of the consequences. The result was to unite Catholic Ireland against them, completing the job begun by the Easter Week executions. The British effectively handed the political initiative to Sinn Féin and completed the discrediting of the Home Rulers. While Sinn Féin took the lead in opposing conscription (with the blessing of the Catholic Church) and the volunteers prepared for armed resistance, it was the labour movement that made the most effective demonstration of opposition. On 20 April 1918, the ITUC held a conference, attended by some 1500 delegates, to discuss the threat of conscription. The conference called a 24-hour general strike for 23 April. Despite the short notice. the stoppage was a complete success everywhere except Belfast and the

Protestant North. It was an unprecedented display of the strength of the Irish labour movement, by now more than fully recovered from the effects of the Dublin Lockout. The importance of the general strike should not be underestimated: it was the first general strike against the War. As Arthur Mitchell points out, the anti-conscription campaign served as 'a demonstration of the power labour could wield when it took the lead in furthering national causes', while according to Emmet O'Connor, it 'shifted the entire nationalist community to the left'.[60] For many labour activists this shift involved at least a rhetorical embrace of the Bolshevik Revolution in Russia with talk of socialism and of the Workers' Republic becoming increasingly widespread and red flags becoming obligatory on demonstrations. Plans and preparations were made for further industrial action when the British actually tried to implement conscription. A railway strike and local general strikes, including a protracted general strike in Dublin were mooted.[61] If it had come to a confrontation then there is every likelihood that British repression would have escalated the conflict, provoking increasing radicalisation. The War of Independence would have begun with mass working-class struggle. This was not to be. Instead, the War ended with German military collapse and revolution in Berlin and Vienna instead. Nevertheless, the labour movement had played a vital role in the crisis with its representatives taking part in the Mansion House conference called by the Lord Mayor of Dublin and with William O'Brien appointed one of the three members of its standing committee along with Eamon de Valera and the Home Rule leader, John Dillon. The strong position that the labour movement achieved in the course of the anti-conscription campaign was soon to be thrown away.

The Irish Labour Party approached the general election of December 1918 with its most radical manifesto, a manifesto that was in many ways an Irish echo of the Bolshevik Revolution. It proclaimed the party's objective as being: 'To win for the workers of Ireland, collectively, the ownership and control of the whole produce of their labour. To secure the democratic management and control of all industries and services by the whole body of workers, manual and mental, engaged therein'.[62] In the event, at a special conference held on 1 November the delegates accepted an executive proposal not to stand candidates by an overwhelming 96 votes to 23. This fateful decision was bitterly opposed by a militant minority led by Thomas Farren and Cathal O' Shannon, but to no avail. The party had surrendered to Sinn Féin pressure. The consequence of this momentous decision was that there was no labour representation in the revolutionary Dáil, that labour had no voice in the revolutionary movement that was to challenge British rule. The national cause had been voluntarily surrendered to Sinn Féin, to a party that was dominated by men who had little sympathy for the working class, for the trade unions or for socialism.

A number of reasons have been put forward to account for the decision to withdraw: fear of alienating the Protestant working class (in fact, of course, Protestant Labour candidates actually did stand in Belfast, securing an average 22 per cent of the poll), a self-sacrificing willingness to give way so the general election could become a referendum on the question of the Republic, and fear that the party would actually go down to a crushing defeat at the hands of Sinn Féin. More important, however, was the unwillingness of the leadership to wholeheartedly commit the movement to a revolutionary challenge to British rule. Such a commitment would have involved considerable risks: Labour, for example, would almost certainly have been banned along with Sinn Féin. The truth was that Johnson, O'Brien and co were not revolutionaries and in the end they bowed to Sinn Féin pressure as a way of getting themselves off the hook on which Connolly's actions in 1916 had impaled them. Their cautious moderation was reinforced by the vociferous demands of Sinn Féin supporters within the labour movement that Sinn Féin should be left a free run against the Home Rulers. This need not have been the case. There can be little doubt that Labour could have used the threat to stand candidates across the country to secure a clear run for itself in Dublin. A Labour Party wholeheartedly committed to the republican cause might well have lost some support but would have won over others and, moreover, would have been considerably better placed in a future independent Ireland. While Brian Farrell goes too far when he regrets the Labour leadership's failure to recognise that they could have 'captured' Sinn Féin and turned it into 'a socialist sword', he is surely closer to the mark when he laments their failure to play an independent part in the revolutionary struggle.[63]

When the revolutionary Dáil met towards the end of January 1919, it proceeded to make a nominal gesture towards Labour. Johnson was asked to draft the new Republic's social statement, the Democratic Programme. Initially, in his draft, he looked to Pearse for inspiration rather than to Connolly, repeating his Jacobin declaration in *The Sovereign People* that 'the nation's sovereignty extends not only to the men and women of the nation but to all the material possessions of the nation…In other words no private right to property is good against the public right of the nation'. He claimed, moreover, 'the right of the nation's citizens to an adequate share of the produce of the nation's labour'. This general statement of the rights and obligations of the risen nation was accompanied by more specific, more controversial, more Connollyite commitments: 'to encourage the organisation of people into trade unions and cooperative societies with a view to the control and administration of the industries by the workers engaged in the industries'. It went on to commit the Republic to the 'elimination of the class in society which lives upon the wealth produced by the workers of the nation but gives no useful service in return', and to 'bring freedom to all who have hitherto been caught in the toils of economic servitude'.[64]

In effect, Johnson was proposing to commit the new state to building up the strength of the labour movement and to recognition of itself as a transitional stage on the road to the emancipation of the working class and the Workers' Republic. As Joseph Lee somewhat pompously observes, this 'was an attempt to foist on the Dáil a programme that had never been presented to the electorate', although in all honesty the Labour leadership regarded it as no more than recognition of the labour movement's contribution to the national cause, as payment for their decision not to stand in the general election.[65]

In the event, Johnson's draft was far too leftwing for Sinn Féin. It was to be a very different document, drawn up by Sean T. O'Kelly, a future President of Ireland, that was adopted by the Dáil on 21 January. The Democratic Programme, as adopted, remained a Jacobin statement, but gone were the support for trade unionism and cooperation and for the ending of 'economic servitude'. Instead, there was a commitment 'to promote the development of the Nation's resources…and to adopt all measures for the recreation and invigoration of our industries'. The new Republic was to seek international agreement on measures to improve the lot of the working class.[66] Even this version was to remain empty rhetoric, designed to enlist working class support in the coming struggle, rather than committing the government to any improvement in the working-class position in Irish society.

The second wave

The historiography of the Irish labour movement has traditionally focussed on Connolly, Larkin and the ITGWU up until 1916. Only recently, however, has attention begun to shift to the post-1917 period, to what can usefully be characterised as the second wave of Irish syndicalism. The period from 1917 to 1923 saw an explosion of militancy and trade union organisation that exceeded in geographic spread and was more protracted than that of the earlier period. It has, nevertheless, been generally ignored. Both F. S. L. Lyons and John Murphy's early surveys of modern Irish history are altogether innocent of the phenomenon and the same is true of more recent surveys such as those by Ronan Fanning, Joseph Lee and Dermot Keogh. The eventual defeat of the second wave seems to have been so complete as to have excised it from national history.[67] Even E. Rumpf and A. C. Hepburn's *Nationalism and Socialism in Twentieth Century Ireland* missed the second wave.[68] Hopefully Emmet O'Connor's path-breaking *Syndicalism in Ireland 1917–1923* has made such neglect no longer possible.

Trade union membership affiliated to the ITUC increased from under 100,000 in 1916 to 225,000 in 1920. The number of trades councils grew from fifteen in 1918 to forty-six in 1921. Leading the way was the ITGWU that increased its membership from 14,000 in 1917 to over 120,000 in 1920. In O'Connor's words: 'Trade unionism exploded in all directions... it assimilated the aggressive class consciousness fermenting since 1914, and the unprecedented frequency of strikes during these years consolidated an exceptionally assertive spirit at the base of the movement'. The workers 'spontaneously revived and developed pre-war Larkinite tactics' and looked forward to the Workers' Republic. It was a 'syndicalist moment'.[69]

One of the remarkable features of this upsurge was the spread of trade union organisation to groups of workers hitherto too weak or too difficult to organise. The key group here were the agricultural workforce who rallied to the ITGWU in their thousands. A census of ITGWU members in June 1918 revealed that of the 43,788 total, 9,634 were agricultural workers.[70] Efforts were made to organise domestic workers.[71] And there were even trade union stirrings among the police.[72] In times of general working-class advance, weak sections are able to win victories that would have been impossible in different circumstances. In March 1918, for example, Dublin barmen won union recognition and a pay rise after defeating a lockout. Another feature of the period was the local general strike. These demonstrations of solidarity took place in fourteen different towns, although in some of them more than once, Charleville, for example, had five general strikes. Moreover, this industrial conflict had an important political dimension.

For Greaves, the architects of the movement were William O'Brien, Cathal O'Shannon and Thomas Johnson. He endorses their political stand as part of the left of the Socialist International as opposed to that taken by Jim Larkin, who was a founder member of the Communist Labor Party in the United States. This is perhaps somewhat surprising from a lifelong communist, but Greaves emphasises the Bolshevik rhetoric that these men were capable of using when they felt it necessary. O'Shannon could quite bluntly declare that 'the Soviet idea was the only one that would confer freedom on Ireland'. Their actions, however, never lived up to their rhetoric.[73] Indeed, rather than O'Brien and O'Shannon leading the movement, a good case can be made that they rode it. The second wave was the product of a working- class revolt and the ITGWU leadership often adopted a revolutionary language in order to retain control over it. Their object was to build up a strong trade union movement rather than to overthrow the social order. They were always social democrats, never communists.[74]

While there was a high level of militancy, accompanied by revolutionary rhetoric and the parading of red flags, to what extent did this amount to a real socialist challenge? Was the movement really only about securing wage improvements or did it have the potential to change Irish society?[75] To pose these alternatives this way shows a misunderstanding of the relationship between labour revolt and the struggle for socialism. It seeks to freeze opinion in order to assess its degree of radicalism at any one moment, rather than recognising that the key to understanding such periods is acknowledging their dynamism, the dynamic interaction between political and economic demands, and how this carries the movement forward. Rosa Luxemburg provides the best account of this process in her *The Mass Strike*.[76] What is clear with regard to the situation is Ireland is that at every point where the movement could have been carried forward, the leadership did their best to contain it.

The Limerick General Strike of April 1919 provides a useful instance of this. The strike began on 14 April in protest against the implementation of British Defence of the Realm Act regulations. As Liam Cahill has shown, working-class consciousness in the city can be characterised as radical rather than socialist, as evidenced by the contents of the *Bottom Dog* newspaper. Nevertheless, militant action was taken, confronting the British authorities, and with the town in the hands of the strike committee which was known locally as 'the soviet'. There was clearly the potential for the struggle to develop in a socialist direction. It is worth remembering in this respect that in February 1917 when the first soviets were established in Petrograd, their consciousness too can be described as radical rather than socialist, but months of struggle was to change that. What happened in Limerick was that the strike committee's call for solidarity, for a national general strike in their support, was ignored by the ITUC, which instead recommended the evacuation of the city as a protest. Rather than extend the struggle, the ITUC acted to keep it localised and, having kept it localised, presided over its defeat in detail. Indeed, defeat was preferable to spreading and intensifying the struggle.[77]

One other point worth noting about the situation in Limerick is that it once again provides evidence of the Catholicism of the Irish working-class. Ruth Russell wrote of how when she 'broke through the military cordon about the proclaimed city of Limerick' she found a ' Soviet supported by the Catholic Church'. When she asked Bishop Fogarty if this indicated that the people were 'priest-ridden', he replied that it was perhaps 'the other way about'. She describes, with obvious surprise, how the workers' guards got to their feet when 'St. Munchin's chapel bell struck for the Angelus' and blessed themselves.[78] There was not another European country where this would have been possible. Aodh de Blacam acknowledged as much when he wrote that 'Catholic communities are generally hostile to socialism and so the socialistic enthusiasm which ran over Ireland during 1919 surprised and puzzled many. But there the fact was'. Ireland, he argued was never 'more devoutly catholic than today…and yet nowhere was the Bolshevik revolution more sympathetically saluted'.[79] But while de Blacam could argue that 'nowhere was the Bolshevik revolution more sympathetically saluted' than in Ireland, the fact was also that nowhere in Europe was communism in its organised form, a Communist Party, weaker. When the Socialist Party of Ireland became the Communist Party of Ireland on 28 October 1921, it had only twenty active members. At a time when Constance Markiewicz, the Minister of Labour in the revolutionary government was warning her colleagues of the 'imminence of social revolution', the Communist Party was completely without influence and, even with only a handful of members, was nevertheless riven with factionalism.[80] The best militants were either committed to the syndicalism of the ITGWU, to the military activity of the IRA, or to both.

One factor that is often seen as militating against socialist prospects in Ireland is that unlike Tsarist Russia in 1917, the land question had already been solved in Ireland. This is a gross oversimplification.[81] There were two constituencies on the land that could have been won to the socialist cause: the agricultural workers and the small farmers. The ITGWU was to be triumphantly successful in organising the agricultural workers, but the ITUC never succeeded or even tried to organise the small farmers. And yet, agrarian radicalism was developing in may parts of the country, an agrarian radicalism that caused Sinn Féin considerable problems. As Darrell Figgis, a determined republican opponent of social radicalism recalled, 'the revived land agitation presented a problem that the Republican Government could not neglect…Cattle-driving and death-notices accumulated, and led finally to violence of a nature that could not be neglected'. He wrote of how in Co. Roscommon a landowner was driven naked through a fair and in Co. Galway a landowner was shot. The Republican Government, he concluded, 'had to keep the national demand for freedom clear from class issues or be caught in the snare of a class war'.[82]

While it is clear that the Sinn Féin leadership was resolutely opposed to the republican struggle developing a socialist character, nevertheless the labour movement played an important role in the conflict. First of all, many union men and women were actively involved in the War of Independence as republicans, whether it be as Sinn Féin members or as IRA volunteers. Peadar O'Donnell is perhaps the best known of these, working as an ITGWU organiser before joining the IRA.[83] There were many others. Of the six men hanged for the 'Bloody Sunday' of shootings, four were active trade unionists, one of them, Patrick Moran, a leading member of the Grocer's Assistants' Trade Union.[84] On a number of occasions, however, the trade union movement intervened directly in the national struggle.

The Limerick General Strike, a direct challenge to the DORA regulations has already been mentioned. More important was the action taken by dockers and railwaymen. On 20 May 1920, dockers in Dublin refused to unload two ships carrying military equipment and material and were promptly locked out. The action spread to the railways where rail workers refused to carry troops or munitions. In many parts of the country, rail transport came to a halt. Only after a protracted dispute did the ITUC call off the boycott in December 1920, effectively surrendering and leaving some 1,500 of the most militant rail workers victimised. According to Charles Townshend, the boycott had 'created severe difficulties, which could have become acute'. Indeed, he goes so far as to suggest that 'if the embargo had been made total in scope and indefinite in duration, it is hard to see how a functional military presence in the hinterland could have been maintained'.[85] Once again, an opportunity was missed. On another occasion, in February 1921, following the fatal shooting of three railwaymen by the police at Mallow, County Cork, the British trade union, the Associated Society of Locomotive Engineers and Firemen (ASLEF), threatened a national strike, embracing both Ireland and Britain. The union never acted on its threats.[86]

Most important as an indication of what might have been was the indefinite general strike called by the ITUC for 13 April 1920 in support of hunger strikers, who included a number of trade union prisoners, in Mountjoy Prison. With support growing and self-proclaimed soviets being established in many towns, the authorities backed down after two days and released the prisoners. Emmet O'Connor quotes the *Manchester Guardian*: 'it is no exaggerations to trace a flavour of proletarian dictatorship about some aspects of the strike'. While he goes on to warn against any equation of 'Irish red flaggery and Russian Bolshevism', he nevertheless concedes 'the extraordinary class triumphalism that had gripped the people'. What had emerged at this time was 'a consciousness that was not revolutionary of itself, but which signified the emergence of a political culture based on the wages movement and outside the formal consensus of the day. The counter-politics stood for the rejection of capitalism, and the celebration of solidarity, spontaneity, and direction'.[87] Now, he is certainly correct that this level of working-class activity and consciousness cannot be equated with October 1917, but what took place in Russia was part of a revolutionary process that had been developing since February. What happened in Ireland in April 1920 can be usefully seen as part of a revolutionary process comparable with but not the same as early stages in the development of the Russian Revolution. In Ireland, however, the movement never developed into a socialist challenge for power. There are, of course, a number of reasons for this, but one of them is certainly the way in which the ITUC leadership was able to contain the movement.

Conor Kostick, in his account of the April 1920 general strike, states quite bluntly that it 'revealed that Irish Workers had the power to defeat British rule'. This goes too far. While it is clear that the struggle in Ireland could have been given a mass character that it would have very difficult for the British to suppress, nevertheless victory was not ensured. Russia had its 1905 as well as its 1917. The general strike showed, however, that the struggle could have developed in a way that would have put Kostick's assertion to the test. The British release of the hunger strikers certainly indicated that the prospect of the working class as a class becoming actively involved in the struggle was not something they would welcome. Paradoxically, it was just as unwelcome to the leaders of Sinn Féin and of the ITUC.[88] One other area of working-class support for the republican struggle that requires mention are the activities of the Irish-American workers, particularly of the New York dockers and of John Fitzpatrick and the Chicago Federation of Labour. On 27 August 1920 in New York, dockers began a boycott of British ships that saw British seamen join the strike. The boycott lasted for three weeks.[89] At the same time, the Chicago Federation of Labor was campaigning within the American Federation of Labor for a boycott of British goods, only to be outmanoeuvred by Samuel Gompers.[90]

While Irish labour undoubtedly suffered from British repression, nevertheless it emerged from the War of Independence stronger than ever before. To a considerable extent, its strength derived from the revolutionary conditions that had existed in the country, but now it faced a new challenge. Employers were determined to push back the advance of trade unionism and were fully supported in this resolve by the rulers of the new state. In the conditions of economic depression that developed in the course of 1921, a major offensive against the Irish trade union movement and working-class living standards was almost inevitable. Two factors combined to prevent the employers from prosecuting their attack at this time. First, the country became embroiled in the Civil War so that the Free State army and police were too heavily committed to fighting the IRA to be able to play an effective strikebreaking role. And secondly, the trade union rank and file offered a degree of resistance that was determined and militant enough to hold what they had. Disputes in the countryside were increasingly accompanied by violence and sabotage, while in the towns workers resorted to occupation as a tactic. During the course of 1922 there were to be some eighty soviets proclaimed, all disowned by the official movement, although local union organisers often played a leading role. Large numbers of workers were involved in seizing control of their workplaces and in many instances keeping production going. The high point of the occupation movement was in May when the Cleeve company locked out its workforce, who proceeded to take control of the creameries, mills and other plants. These occupations only ended in August with the arrival of Free State troops in the Suir valley.[91]

Once the Free State had effectively defeated its republican opponents, it quickly proceeded to the restoration of property rights and employers' prerogatives, deploying troops and police to break strikes and impose wage cuts. Indeed, the government itself quite deliberately led the way by imposing wage cuts on postal workers with the intention of provoking a strike. Even before the dispute began, the Postmaster General James J. Walsh had approached the British Postmaster General to ask for assistance in recruiting strikebreakers from among the Irish Workers in the British Post Office. Walsh was himself a former postman and militant trade unionist before his rise to prominence first in Sinn Féin and now in Cumann na nGaedheal. He set about breaking the strike with a vengeance. The postal workers struck on 10 September, in defiance of a declaration that their action was illegal. Troops and police attacked pickets, beating men and women, and strenuous efforts were made to recruit strikebreakers. With the government determined to break the strike and without any solidarity action from other groups of workers, the unions admitted defeat on 29 September. They had assurances from President Cosgrave that there would be no victimisation, but Walsh refused to be bound by these. Not only were union members victimised, but Walsh also treated the strike as a break in service with serious consequences for pension rights and incremental rates. As the unions bitterly complained, not even the British had done this when they had supported the April 1920 general strike. Moreover, Walsh was quite clear about the implications of the dispute, remarking that 'at this critical juncture to smash such a well organised strike was a salutary lesson to the general indiscipline which has just seemed to run riot through the land'.[92] Private employers hastened to follow his lead.

The trade union movement suffered crushing defeats in the course of 1923. The decisive battle was the six-month Waterford farm workers strike that began on 17 May and was only called off on 8 December. The strikers held out in the face of severe repression carried out by troops, police and armed vigilantes, but in the end they went down to total defeat. The ITGWU in County Waterford ceased to exist and agrarian trade unionism throughout Ireland went into catastrophic decline.[93] The battering the movement received was made all the worse by the bitter divisions within the ITGWU, divisions that were exacerbated when Jim Larkin finally returned from the United States at the end of April 1923. He mounted a strong challenge to William O'Brien's leadership of the union. How far was this a matter of personalities? How far was it a question of politics? In his history of the ITGWU, Greaves is contemptuously dismissive of Larkin: he was a fantasist, completely out of touch, his behaviour 'cannot be excused on any grounds' and, most incredibly, his 'egoism' had created the situation 'in which the employers could launch their general offensive with the certainty of success'.[94]

While personalities undoubtedly came into the conflict between the two men and their supporters, far more important were questions of strategy: how to respond to the employers' offensive? O'Brien favoured retreat and attempts to reach an accommodation, while Larkin favoured militant resistance. In effect, Larkin took on the role of a rank and file leader in Dublin, leading both the resistance to the employers and an insurgency against O'Brien's leadership within the union. His stance had the support of the overwhelming majority of the Dublin membership. Elsewhere in the country, rank and file traditions were not so strong and O'Brien was able to retain control through the agency of the union's paid organisers. Larkin had no intention of starting a breakaway union. That decision was taken prematurely by his brother Peter, a man much closer to the IWW tradition than Larkin himself, while he was in Moscow.[95] Regardless of Peter Larkin's action in establishing the Workers Union of Ireland, it is certain that O'Brien would have made good his expulsion of Larkin and his supporters so that the outcome was really only a matter of timing. Moreover, a good case can be made that regardless of either Larkin brother some sort of breakaway from O'Brien's bureaucratic rule was on the cards. Such was to be the experience in London and Glasgow where dockers had to deal with Ernest Bevin's Transport and General Workers Union. The Workers Union was established on 15 June 1924, taking with it two thirds of the ITGWU's Dublin membership, but only twenty-three of the 300 provincial branches. O'Brien proceeded to ally with the employers against the new union.[96]

The catastrophic decline of the Irish trade union movement was certainly not due to Larkin or the establishment of the Workers' Union. In 1926, the ITGWU still claimed to have 40,000 members, but by 1929 this had collapsed to only 15,000. The decline of the ITUC was equally dramatic with membership falling to 92,000 in 1929. While this was undoubtedly due to the economic circumstances, an important part was also played by the unremitting hostility of the Cosgrave government. As for Larkin, there was now no labour revolt for him to become the voice of. He was reduced to the leadership of a small, embattled union that was successfully contained by the employers together with his enemies in the trade union movement led by William O'Brien. Larkin's figure still looms large, however, and this has led to him being blamed for, among other things, the failure of Irish communism. In a recent article, Emmet O'Connor has argued that he deliberately set out to prevent the development of an Irish Communist Party and he puts this down, at least in part, to Larkin's acute personality problems.[97] This is not convincing. First of all, Larkin had been a founder of the Communist Labor Party in the United States so that, whatever his political weaknesses, he was clearly prepared to be part of a collective leadership where it appeared that the movement could actually be built. Given this, it is much more likely that he recognised that a communist party could not be built, at this time, in Ireland. His Dublin-based Irish Workers' League was not an obstacle to building a communist party, but all that could be built in the situation he found himself in, a situation where, unlike America, he was very much a one-man band whether he liked it or not. What is remarkable is how much Larkin was actually able to hold together, at great personal cost, rather than what he failed to achieve.[98]

The vision of trade unionism that triumphed in Ireland was to be that given expression by William O'Brien as early as August 1918:

> Let us get our fully equipped offices, let us man them with the best men and women either love or money can buy; let our officials be highly skilled, well trained, able, and where necessary, experts and specialists in their particular lines, and let us adopt all the best and most up-to-date methods of conducting business. For the conduct of the movement is, to a certain degree a great business, and we must have it managed on business lines.[99]

It was only to triumph in the conditions of defeat that overwhelmed the movement in 1923.

Notes

1. Marcel van der Linden and Wayne Thorpe (eds), *Revolutionary Syndicalism. An international perspective* (Aldershot, 1990); Chris Wrigley (ed.), *Challenges of Labour. Central and Western Europe, 1917–1920* (London, 1993); Sam Davies et al. (eds), *Dock Workers* (Aldershot, 2000).
2. Emmet O'Connor, *Syndicalism in Ireland 1917–1923* (Cork, 1988).
3. See in particular Bob Holton, *British Syndicalism* (London, 1976).
4. For social conditions in Dublin see Joseph V. O'Brien, *Dear, Dirty Dublin* (Los Angeles, 1982), and Mary Daly, *Dublin: the Deposed Capital* (Cork, 1984).
5. Arnold Wright, *Disturbed Dublin* (London, 1914), pp.2–3.
6. *Irish Worker*, 17 August 1912. For the Savoy Confectionery lockout, see *Irish Worker*, 5, 12, 19, 26 July, 9 and 16 August 1913.
7. The standard biography of Jim Larkin is still Emmet Larkin, *James Larkin* (London, 1977), but see also my '"A Lamp to Guide Your Feet": Jim Larkin, the Irish Worker and the Dublin working class', *European History Quarterly*, vol. 20, no. 1 (1990), and the special issue of *Saothar*, devoted to Larkin: Saothar, 4 (1978).
8. See John Gray, *City in Revolt: James Larkin and the Belfast Dock Strike of 1907* (Belfast, 1985).
9. See C. Desmond Greaves, *The Irish Transport and General Workers' Union. The formative years* (Dublin, 1982).
10. For the Irish Women Workers' Union, see Mary Jones, *These Obstreperous Lassies. A history of the Irish Women Workers' Union* (Dublin, 1988).
11. William Kenefick, *Rebellious and Contrary. The Glasgow dockers 1853–1932* (East Linton, 2000), pp.200–4 and 210–12.
12. See Robert G. Lowery, 'Sean O'Casey and the *Irish Worker*', in Robert G. Lowery (ed.), *O'Casey Annual* 3 (London, 1984), and see my 'A Lamp to Guide Your Feet'.
13. Lord Askwith, *Industrial Problems and Disputes* (London, 1920), p.113.
14. Larkin, *James Larkin*, p.145.
15. *Irish Worker*, 24 May 1924.
16. Wright, *Disturbed Dublin*, p.255.
17. Askwith, *Industrial Problems*, p.259.
18. Holton, *British Syndicalism*, pp.207–8. For an alternative view, see Dermot Keogh, *The Rise of the Irish Working Class 1890–1914* (Belfast, 1982).
19. See John W. Boyle, *The Irish Labour Movement in the Nineteenth Century* (Washington, 1988), and Emmet O'Connor, *A Labour History of Ireland 1824–1960* (Dublin, 1992), and my own *Fenianism in Mid-Victorian Britain* (London, 1994).
20. See Leon O Broin, *Revolutionary Underground* (Dublin, 1976).
21. *Irish Worker*, 27 May 1911.
22. *Irish Worker*, 15 July 1911.
23. See my 'James Connolly and the Easter Rising', Science and Society, vol. XLVII,

no. 2, (1978), and my 'In the hunger-cry of the nation's poor is heard the voice of Ireland: Sean O'Casey and politics', *Journal of Contemporary History*, vol. 20, no. 2 (1985).
24. See my 'As Catholic as the Pope: James Connolly and the Roman Catholic Church in Ireland', *Saothar*, 11 (1986) and, more recently, Fintan Lane, 'James Connolly's 1901 census return', *Saothar*, 25 (2000).
25. *Irish Worker*, 20 September 1913.
26. For William Martin Murphy see Thomas Morrissey S. J., *William Martin Murphy* (Dundalk, 1997), and Andy Bielenberg, 'Entrepreneurship, power and public opinion in Ireland: the career of William Martin Murphy', *Irish Economic and Social History*, XVII (2000).
27. Pádraig Yeates, *Lockout Dublin 1913* (Dublin, 2000).
28. See my 'The devil it was who sent Larkin to Ireland: *The Liberator*, Larkinism and the Dublin Lockout of 1913', *Saothar*, 18 (1993), and my 'The curse of Larkinism: Patrick McIntyre, *The Toiler* and the Dublin Lockout', *Eire-Ireland*, vol. XXX, no. 3 (1995).
29. Yeates, *Lockout Dublin*, pp.434-5.
30. See Holton, *British Syndicalism*, pp.192-4, Keith Harding, 'The co-operative commonwealth: Ireland, Larkin and the *Daily Herald*' in Stephen Yeo (ed.), *New Views of Co-operation* (London, 1988), and Bill Moran, '1913, Jim Larkin and the British labour movement', *Saothar*, 4 (1978).
31. R. M. Fox, *Smokey Crusade* (London, 1938), p.172.
32. *Forward*, 9 February 1914.
33. See my 'Connolly and his biographers', *Irish Political Studies*, 5 (1990), for a discussion.
34. R. M. Fox, *Jim Larkin. The rise of underman* (London, 1957); Emmet Larkin, *James Larkin*; Jim Larkin, *In the Footsteps of Big Jim* (Dublin, 1995), and Donal Nevin (ed.), *James Larkin, Lion of the Fold* (Dublin, 1998). Emmet O'Connor has a new biography forthcoming.
35. See *The Attempt to Smash The Irish Transport and General Workers' Union* (Dublin, 1924).
36. Greaves, *The ITGWU*, p.131.
37. David Krause, *The Letters of Sean O'Casey* (New York, 1980), p.347.
38. For Larkin in America see Manus O'Riordan, 'Larkin in America: the road to Sing Sing' in Nevin, *James Larkin* and Claire Culleton, 'James Larkin and J. Edgar Hoover: Irish politics and American conspiracy', *Eire-Ireland*, XXXV, (Fall-Winter 2000-2001), p.3-4.
39. Richard English, *Radicals and the Republic* (Oxford, 1994), p.19.
40. *Rossa Souvenir*, July 1915.
41. *Workers Republic*, 5 February 1916.
42. On 25 April 1915, the 2nd Dublin Fusiliers lost 510 men killed or wounded in an attack on St. Julien on the Western Front. During the fighting, the cry went up 'three cheers for Jim Larkin'; Tom Johnstone, *Orange, Green and Khaki* (Dublin, 1992), p.75.

43. See *Sinn Féin Rebellion Handbook* (Dublin, 1917), pp.9–10.
44. F.A. McKenzie, *The Irish Rebellion—What Happened and Why* (Dublin, 1917), pp.60–1, 77.
45. P. O'Cathasaigh, *The Story of the Irish Citizen Army* (Dublin, 1919), pp.51–2.
46. R. M. Fox, *Louie Bennett* (Dublin, 1958), p.47. For a more recent discussion of her attitude towards Connolly, see Rosemary Cullen Owens, *Louie Bennett* (Cork, 2001), pp.65–7.
47. Thomas Johnston, *Memories* (London, 1952), pp.238–9.
48. C. Desmond Greaves, *The Life and Times of James Connolly* (London, 1961), p.420.
49. Greaves, *Life and Times*, pp.384, 425. See also John Hoffman's 'The dialectic between democracy and socialism in the Irish national question' in Austin Morgan and Bob Purdie (eds), *Ireland: Divided nation, divided class* (London, 1980), p.180.
50. W. K. Anderson, *James Connolly and the Irish Left* (Blackrock, 1994), pp.64, 75.
51. See my 'James Connolly, the German Empire and the Great War', *The Irish Sword*, XVI, 65 (Winter 1986).
52. David Howell, *A Lost Left* (Manchester, 1986), p.142.
53. Austen Morgan, *James Connolly. A political biography* (Manchester, 1988), pp.139–95.
54. Annie Smithson, *Myself—And Others* (Dublin, 1944), p.271.
55. Piaras F. Mac Lochlainn, *Last Words* (Dublin, 1971), p.127.
56. Esther Roper, *Prison Letters of Countess Markiewicz* (London, 1934), pp.27, 73.
57. Greaves, *The ITGWU*, p.174. See also Arthur Mitchell, *Labour in Irish Politics 1890–1930* (Dublin, 1974), pp.75–6.
58. Anderson, *James Connolly*, p.104. For Johnson see also J. Anthony Gaughan, *Thomas Johnson* (Mount Merrion, 1980).
59. Michael Hopkinson, *Green Against Green. The Irish Civil War* (Dublin 1990), pp.45–6.
60. Mitchell, *Labour in Irish Politics*, p.89: Emmet O'Connor, *A Labour History of Waterford* (Waterford, 1989), p.124.
61. David Fitzpatrick, *The Two Irelands 1912–1939* (Oxford, 1998), pp.73–4. See also Thomas Johnson's 'Memorandum to local defence committees' in Gaughan, *Thomas Johnson*, pp.431–5.
62. Michael Laffan, 'Labour must wait: Ireland's conservative revolution' in Patrick J. Corish, *Radicals, Rebels and Establishments* (Belfast, 1985), p.206.
63. Brian Farrell, *The founding of Dáil Èireann* (Dublin, 1971), p.44. For an interesting discussion of the long-term significance of the 1918 decision, see Kieran Allen, *Fianna Fáil and Irish Labour* (London, 1997), pp.6–7.
64. Farrell, *Dáil Èireann*, pp.88–9.
65. Joe Lee, Ireland 1912–1985 (Cambridge, 1989), p.41.
66. Farrell, *Dáil Èireann*, pp.87–8.
67. F. S. L. Lyons, *Ireland Since the Famine* (London, 1971); John Murphy, *Ireland in the Twentieth Century* (Dublin, 1975); Ronan Fanning, *Independent Ireland* (Dublin, 1983); Lee, *Ireland*; Dermot Keogh, *Twentieth Century Ireland* (Dublin, 1994).

68. E. Rumpf and A. C. Hepburn, *Nationalism and Socialism in Twentieth Century Ireland* (Liverpool, 1977). They write that 'If 1913 marked the beginning, then 1916 marked the end of the social revolution in Dublin' (p.20).
69. O'Connor, *Labour History of Ireland*, p.94.
70. There is a growing body of research chronicling the struggles of rural labour: see in particular Dan Bradley, *Farm Labourers. Irish struggle 1900–1976* (Belfast, 1988); John Cunningham, *Labour in the West of Ireland. Working life and struggle 1890–1914* (Belfast, 1995); Ross Connolly, 'A rightful place in the sun—the struggle of the farm and rural labourers of County Wicklow', in Kenny Hannigan and William Nolan (eds), *Wicklow: History and Society* (Dublin, 1994); and O'Connor, *Labour History of Waterford*.
71. John Lynch, *A Tale of Three Cities. Comparative studies in working-class life* (London, 1998), p.30
72. Neligan, *A Spy in the Castle*, pp.54–5.
73. Greaves, *The ITGWU*, pp.235.
74. Adrian Pimley, 'The working-class movement and the Irish Revolution 1896–1923' in D. G. Boyce (ed.), *The Revolution in Ireland 1879–1923* (London, 1988), p.210.
75. See Laffan, 'Labour must wait', pp.209–10.
76. Rosa Luxemburg, *The Mass Strike* (London, 1986 edn).
77. Liam Cahill, *Forgotten Revolution. The Limerick Soviet 1919* (Dublin, 1990).
78. Ruth Russell, *What's The Matter With Ireland?* (New York, 1920), pp.127, 136, 138.
79. Aodh De Blacam, *What Sinn Fein Stands For* (Dublin, 1921), p.105.
80. Mike Milotte, *Communism in Modern Ireland* (Dublin, 1984), pp.49–50.
81. See in particular Paul Bew, 'Sinn Féin, agrarian radicalism and the war of independence 1919–1921' in Boyce, *The Revolution*, and Tony Varley, 'Agrarian crime and social control: Sinn Féin and the land question in the west of Ireland in 1920', in Mike Tomlinson, Tony Varley and Ciraran McCullagh (eds), *Whose Law and Order?* (Belfast, 1988).
82. Darrell Figgis, *Recollections of the Irish War* (London, 1927), pp.292–3.
83. For Peadar O'Donnell's own reminiscences, see his *Monkeys In the Superstructure* (Galway, 1985), but see also Anton McCabe, 'The stormy petrel of the transport workers: Peadar O'Donnell, trade unionist 1917–1920', *Saothar*, 19 (1994) and, more recently, Peter Hegarty, *Peadar O'Donnell* (Cork, 1999) and Donal Ó Drisceoil, *Peadar O'Donnell* (Cork, 2001).
84. Conor Kostik, *Revolution in Ireland. Popular militancy 1917–1923* (London, 1996), p.137.
85. Charles Townshend, 'The Irish railway strike of 1920; industrial action and civil resistance in the struggle for independence', *Irish Historical Studies*, vol. XXI, no. 83 (March 1979), p.281.
86. D. G. Boyce, *Englishmen and Irish Troubles* (London, 1972), pp.68–9.
87. O'Connor, *Syndicalism in Ireland*, p.45. For an interesting account of developments in one particular country see D. R. O'Connor Lysaght, 'County Tipperary: class struggle and national struggle 1916–1924' in William Nolan and Thomas

McGrath (eds), *Tipperary: History and Society* (Dublin, 1985).
88. Kostik, *Revolution*, p.127–8.
89. Joe Doyle, 'Striking for Ireland on the New York Docks', in Ronald Bayer and Timothy Meagher (eds), *The New York Irish* (Baltimore, 1996). See also Bruce Nelson, *Divided We Stand. American workers and the struggle for black equality* (Princeton, 2001), pp.26–31 in particular for the support of African American dockworkers for the Irish cause.
90. Elizabeth McKillen, 'American labor, the Irish Revolution and the campaign for a boycott of British goods 1916–1924', *Radical History Review*, 61 (Winter 1995).
91. See Tom Crean, 'From Petrograd to Bruree', in David Fitzpatrick (ed.), *Revolution? Ireland 1917–1923* (Dublin, 1990).
92. See Alexis Guilbride, 'A scrapping of every principle of individual liberty: the postal strike of 1922', *History Ireland* (Winter 2000), and Kostik, *Revolution*, p.185.
93. See O'Connor, *Labour History of Waterford*, pp.183–208. O'Connor's assessment of the scale of the defeat, both in County Waterford and nationally, is worth noting: 'trade unions entered the Irish state's first full year of peace broken and embittered. The gains in real wages achieved in the later war years and after had largely been swept away in the class war from 1921 to 1923' (p.208).
94. Greaves, *The ITGWU*, p.319.
95. While Jim Larkin had been in the United States during the war, his brother Peter was in Australia, a member of the IWW, actively opposing the war. He fell victim to the suppression of the IWW, and, was one of the 'Sydney Twelve', sentenced to ten years imprisonment for treason in December 1916. He was eventually released in August 1920. See Frank Cain, 'The industrial workers of the world: aspects of its suppression in Australia 1916–1919', *Labour History*, 42 (1982), and Ian Taylor, *Sydney's Burning* (Melbourne, 1967).
96. For a recent account of the split, see Mark Farmer, 'James Larkin and the Workers Union of Ireland', *Études Irlandaises* (2001).
97. Emmet O'Connor, 'Jim Larkin and the Communist Internationals 1923–9', *Irish Historical Studies*, vol. XXXI, no. 123 (May 1999).
98. See my unpublished paper 'The trajectory of Jim Larkin'.
99. Anderson, *James Connolly*, p.153. The lack of a biography of William O'Brien is a fundamental, indeed inexcusable, gap in Irish labour history, but see Arthur Mitchell, 'William O'Brien (1881–1968) and the Irish labour movement', *Studies*, vol. 60, no. 239, (Winter 1971), and D. R. O'Connor Lysaght, 'The rake's progress of a syndicalist: the political career of William O'Brien, Irish Labour leader', *Saothar*, 9 (1983).

Prisoner Number 3566
An interview with Joseph Leon Glazer

Allison Drew

Henry Glazer and Joseph Leon Glazer—father and son—differed sharply in their views of communism. But their lives and their relationships with the communist system in the Soviet Union converged at one important intersection: both were prisoners in the Soviet system of forced labour camps known as the gulag, the Main Directorate for Corrective Labour Camps. Henry Glazer, a communist, was arrested in Moscow in 1935, sentenced to five years and sent to Potma, where, presumably, he died. Joseph was arrested in 1949, sentenced to ten years and sent to Karaganda. He survived and was released in 1957.[1]

It is through the son's words that we know about the father, and it is in the telling of his father's tale, that we learn about the son. Henry Glazer was, to all appearances, a typical South African socialist—and later communist—of the first few decades of the twentieth century. South Africa's first socialists were foreign-born, typically from Eastern Europe or from Britain, and its socialism was an imported doctrine. Like many first-generation socialists, Henry Glazer came from Eastern Europe. Born in Poland, he and his wife Rose left the country of their birth around the turn of the century. They went first to Great Britain in search of a better life. In 1902 they went to South Africa, where Henry Glazer had heard about the gold mines on the Transvaal. The Glazers decided to stay, although they did not, initially, have a stable life. Between 1902 and 1908 Henry Glazer lived in Oudtshoorn, Grahamstown, Bloemfontein and Kimberley. He applied for naturalisation in the Cape Colony in 1907. He subsequently moved to Pietersburg, where he applied for naturalisation in the Transvaal, which was granted in 1909.[2]

His political radicalisation, as far as is known, occurred through the written word. He was inspired by *The Jungle*, a novel published by American socialist Upton Sinclair in 1906. The story of an immigrant Lithuanian worker, the novel exposed the scandalous working and sanitary conditions in the Chicago meat packing industry. It became an instant best seller, arousing a public outcry that culminated in the establishment of the United States Food and Drug Administration and of federal inspection standards for meat. The novel galvanised socialists around the world.

Convinced that socialism was the way forward, Henry Glazer became involved in socialist politics around 1917. He was one of the leaders of the Yiddish-speaking branch of the International Socialist League, which was formed in August 1917. The leaders of this group were mostly artisans and intellectuals; quite a number, including Glazer, were tailors.[3] In July 1921, inspired by the Russian revolution, most of the tiny socialist groups in South Africa merged into the Communist Party of South Africa (CPSA), which affiliated to the Communist International. Glazer was one of these first communists.

Within six months of its formation, the CPSA was catapulted into a labour struggle that transformed South African politics—the 1922 Rand Revolt.[4] Henry Glazer, by then an associate of the popular and respected communist trade union leader W. H. (Bill) Andrews, was involved in this strike. Glazer himself had quite a reputation at the time, being described in the South African press as 'the well-known international socialist'.[5] The Rand Revolt, an armed protest by white workers, was the culmination of fifteen years of labour protests around the country. During the first years of the gold mining industry, white mine workers who had come as skilled craft workers from overseas, enjoyed a monopoly of skilled work in the mines; black workers performed heavy labour classified as unskilled. But industrial developments on the mines led to deskilling. From 1907 higher-priced English-speaking craft workers were replaced by cheaper, unskilled Afrikaners, who protected their new access to skills training and skilled work on the grounds of colour. Over the next decade the Chamber of Mines periodically tried to lower labour costs by replacing whites with cheaper black labour but in 1918 it conceded a Status Quo Agreement that protected white workers in specified jobs from replacement by black workers. Nonetheless, the gold mining industry was hard hit by the global recession which followed the post-war inflationary boom. Between 1920 and 1922 the premium gold price dropped significantly. As the recession deepened, the Chamber of Mines decided to abrogate the Status Quo Agreement, restructure underground work and cut the wages and the numbers of white workers. White trade union leaders saw this as a prelude to either driving down white wages to the level of black workers or eliminating the higher paid white workers from the mines altogether.[6] Although the strike clearly had racist aspects, which the CPSA rejected, it nonetheless supported the efforts of white mine workers to retain their wage levels.[7]

The strike broke out in January 1922. In March the state began using bombs, tanks and machine guns against the civilian population. The strikers were militarily unprepared. A call by communist leader Bill Andrews for a general strike failed to generate adequate support, and there were pogroms against blacks in Johannesburg and elsewhere. On 10 March, the government proclaimed martial law, imprisoning about 1,500 strikers. 'F', a member of the CPSA who worked as a typist for Andrews, was in the party office that day. Half an hour after the proclamation, he wrote to fellow communist David Ivon Jones in Moscow, 'a large posse of mounted police surrounded the Trades Hall. The detectives poured into our office arresting all that were there but myself…I had to look on while they ransacked the office. This time seemed the signal for all the shooting that went on continually for five days throughout the town—aeroplanes, bombs, machine + Louis guns.'[8] The well-known communist Sidney Bunting was arrested on 12 March.[9] Henry Glazer was arrested a day later, 'after a sharp struggle'. The police seized his socialist literature, including Daniel de Leon's *What Means this Strike?* and Karl Radek's *Socialism from Science to Practice*.[10] On 14 March Glazer was sentenced to six months' imprisonment with hard labour for 'obstructing the military'. On 16 March, the strike was called off. Overall, about 230 to 250 people died as a result of violence during the strike. Close to 5000 people were arrested; 46 were charged with murder, of which 18 were sentenced to death and 4 executed.[11] On 28 July, Glazer and 47 others charged with contravening martial law were granted remission on their sentences.[12]

The violent response of the Smuts government to the Rand strike needs to be seen against the backdrop of international working-class struggles: the ripples of the Russian revolution were felt as far away as South Africa by both imperialist interests and organised labour. Newspapers campaigned against Russian immigrants.[13] Both capitalists and communists used the discourse of international socialist revolution, however inaccurately, comparing the Rand Revolt to a Bolshevik-inspired revolt.[14] The judicial enquiry which followed the revolt, however, belied the allegation of a 'communist plot'.[15]

Nonetheless, the state cracked down on communists. Henry Glazer had a hard time making a living after the strike. He gave up tailoring and opened a fish and chip shop. It was not uncommon for socialists, particularly those who had lost their jobs due to a strike, to become self-employed shop owners. Virtually nothing is known of Henry Glazer's life during the next decade aside from what his son Joseph Glazer tells us. But in historiographical terms, Henry Glazer's experiences are important. Most accounts of South Africa's socialist movement focus on organisational officials and party cadres and their experiences of repression.[16] That so little is known of Henry Glazer's life itself indicates how little we actually know about the history of South African socialism and of the workers' movement once we move beyond its better-known personalities. Glazer's life tells us about those socialists who, while not leaders, were nonetheless victimised by the state as a result of their involvement in the Rand Revolt. It also gives us more understanding about the range of options available to South Africans during the great depression.

Henry Glazer was unique amongst South African socialists in one crucial respect. He is the only known socialist who voluntarily left South Africa to emigrate to the Soviet Union in the 1930s. A few of the early socialists born in the Russian Empire returned to the Soviet Union in the early 1920s. Other South African communists and trade unionists went to the Soviet Union in the 1920s and 1930s. Some went to represent the South African affiliate at congresses of the Communist International; some went to study at the Lenin School or the Communist University for Eastern Toilers in Moscow; still others were invited by the Soviet government to see the wonders built by the world's first socialist state. And in 1937 a small number of South African communists were summoned to Moscow by the Comintern Executive to account for what it saw as problems and deviations in the South African affiliate. Three of those communists were later arrested.[17]

But Henry Glazer's story is different. He did not go to the Soviet Union on behalf of the CPSA or as a member of a trade union delegation. As his son recounts, he was inspired by Stalin's call to socialists around the world to help build the Soviet state and develop its industries. But his decision was made against the backdrop of the great depression that had swept across the world and into South Africa. In the early 1930s rural poverty swept both blacks and whites into towns, hoping for work. Small-scale Afrikaner farmers lost their land and took up factory work, or sent family members to town to stave off complete proletarianisation. In towns, they came into direct competition with black workers, who were also streaming in from the reserves. The urban white working class was also economically ravaged in the 1930s. In 1932 the Carnegie Commission published the findings of its study of poor whites—a joint project financed by the Carnegie Corporation of New York, the South African government and the Dutch Reformed Church. The government's response was to implement a programme of state-led job creation for whites.[18] Had Henry Glazer remained in South Africa, he would have been one of the beneficiaries of the reforms implemented by the South African state to alleviate what was known as the poor white problem. But he chose to leave South Africa in search of the new socialist society and, no doubt, of a better life.

Henry Glazer's story has come to our attention through his son's story.

Joseph Leon Glazer was born in 1916 in South Africa, the youngest of four boys. He still recalls the early days in Johannesburg, before he accompanied his father to the Soviet Union. These were the years of schoolboy games and of silent films, pastimes familiar to other white boys growing up in the working-class areas of Johannesburg. Eleven years older than Joseph Glazer, Bernard Sachs' memoir of his boyhood in Johannesburg recalls those silent films—'doubly exciting because of the musical accompaniment', which, 'hackneyed and indifferently played most of the time, was like summer rain after a long drought and brought back a spiritual warmth which seemed to have departed for ever.'[19]

An adventurous boy, Joseph Glazer tells us that he eagerly accepted his father's invitation to come along to Moscow. On their departure from South Africa they were moved up from third- to second-class accommodation— in a typically South African episode—which the father saw as a good omen. It was a long year's journey. But Joseph Glazer had an eerie presentiment that something was not right, once they crossed the border into the Soviet Union. They entered the Soviet Union around December 1932, as the terror was unfolding and as xenophobia was on the rise.

In 1934 Rose Glazer and two of her sons, Michael and Aubrey (Abraham), came to visit. Henry Glazer would have been around sixty years old by then. There is a photograph of Henry and Rose in Sokolniki Park, around May 1934, both dressed in Russian clothes. But Rose decided that the Soviet Union was not for her, as did Michael, who did not like the country at all, and who cried out 'Whoopee', Joseph Glazer recalls, as the train pulled out of Moscow.[20] There is another photograph of Henry Glazer, which was found in his KGB file. It shows a man greatly aged, his facial expression disoriented, his eyes staring in terror, his hair in disarray. It is obvious that he has been tortured.

Joseph Glazer was imprisoned at Karaganda in northern Kazakhstan. The author Aleksandr Solzhenitsyn was also a prisoner there; Karaganda was the setting of his novel, *One Day in the Life of Ivan Denisovich*.[21] There are two photographs of Joseph Glazer at Karaganda. In one, he is standing on his own, outside. Surprisingly, he does not seem to be wearing his obligatory prison number; perhaps he had taken off his jacket and cap. Then another photo: a group of Polish prisoners sitting around a table. Joseph is there as well. It was a Polish celebration, and Joseph was invited because of his parentage. He also had another photograph while in prison, a photograph of his daughter, by then a little girl, which had been smuggled into the camp.[22] She had been born three months after his arrest, during the period of his interrogation in Moscow; his interrogator had told him that the baby was a boy. It was only years later, when he received this photograph, that he found out that his child was a girl.

Post-Soviet Russia prefers not to look back at this horrific part of its history—the history of the gulag. The Communist Party of the Russian Federation has failed to come to terms with its own past, preferring as one critic put it, 'promises for the future' rather than 'responsibility for the past'.[23] Its leader, Gennady Zyuganov, has called on Russians 'to avoid those grim historical pages' and instead to 'consider the victory over Hitler, and Stalin's role in that victory'. Indeed, he has failed to acknowledge that political repression and forced labour continued into the postwar era. 'As for the repressions', he has stated, 'they were denounced in the 1950s.' He has claimed as well: 'I was raised after the war, and in my time there have been no repressions.'[24] But not only were millions, like Joseph Glazer, imprisoned in the gulag in the 1940s and 1950s, forced labour camps for political prisoners continued to exist in the Soviet Union until the late 1980s. Perm 36, a camp in a remote area of the Urals, opened in 1972 and finally closed down in 1987.[25]

The left, too, prefers not to examine this horrific part of its own history. Research on the gulag pales in comparison to the quantities of research and writing on forced labour and extermination camps in Nazi Germany. The history of socialism has many inspirational moments. But the stories of Henry Glazer and Joseph Glazer are those of ordinary people whose names are not usually found in history books but whose lives became entangled with the dark underside of the socialist movement and who can therefore help us to understand the tragic aspects of twentieth-century socialism.

The interview took place at Podolsk, Russia on 22 September 2001.

AD What do you remember about your parents and about your childhood in South Africa?

JG Both my parents came from Poland. My father, Henry Glazer, was born in 1874 in Lask. My mother, Rose Kamelgam, was born in 1881 in Lodz. At some point my father moved to Lodz and there my parents met and were married. They left Poland around 1902 or 1903. My dad loved travelling around the world, and he left Poland for Britain in search of a better life. Then in Britain he heard about the gold mines in South Africa and went there. And so my brothers and I were all born in South Africa. My oldest brother was Barney, then Aubrey, and then Michael, who was born in 1910. I was the last, born in 1916 in the General Hospital in Ellis Park, Doornfontein, a suburb of Johannesburg.

My first remembrances are of the street where we had a house. This house was right in the centre of Johannesburg, on Simmonds Street. When my dad arrived in South Africa he and my mother had lived in one town but then they moved to Johannesburg and decided to remain. When my parents were living in Doornfontein, my brothers went to the government school in Doornfontein, on Davies Street. So my parents also decided to send me to this school. So I went to this government school in Doornfontein and studied there until the very day that I left for the Soviet Union. My daily route from Simmonds Street to the school was first on the tram, then across the pedestrian railway bridge.

I liked sports and played rugby, cricket and kenneki, a South African game that is played with two sticks. One of our teachers, Mr Jacobs, used to take us to the open air swimming pool in his Chevrolet. He loved hearing us sing Afrikaans.

I loved going to the bioscope. At first, before 1927, there were only silent films. My friend and I used to go to the bioscope and watch films. I loved cowboy films in which featured Tom Mix, Gary Cooper and William S. Hart. At the bioscopes, you were expected to order food while you were watching the films. Because they were silent, you could make noise, munch and chew. I would order pastries and ice creams. But sometimes I would sit at a table with empty plates that had been left by other customers, pretending to have bought something. That way, I could see the films free of charge! In 1927, if I am not mistaken, sound films came to South Africa. I used to see sound films at the Bijou Cinema. I saw 'The singing fool', featuring Al Jolson, who sang 'Climb upon my knee sonny boy'.[26] I preferred musicals and comedies rather than dramas. I was brought up to prefer happy endings.

I remember the first time I saw snow. It was 1926, and I was about 10 years old. My brothers and I were very happy and made a snowman in the yard, rolling balls and putting one ball on top of the other. We used coal for his eyes. But when we woke up in the morning, there was nothing left of our snowman! I couldn't understand where he had disappeared. When I came to this country, it was winter. There was plenty, plenty of snow on the ground, and I thought to myself, 'Will the snow ever melt?'.

AD Do you know how your father came to join the Communist Party of South Africa?

JG My dad was a member of the Johannesburg Public Library. One day he read a book by the American novelist Upton Sinclair, called *The Jungle*. This book was about the slaughterhouses in Chicago and of the conditions of the people who worked in the slaughterhouses. This book transformed my father's views about the world and about the conditions of the working class. In such a manner he became a communist. He was one of the first to organise the working class in South Africa. In 1922 my father, together with Mr Bunting, also a communist, organised the miners' strike. My father was very active in politics.

I used to go to the Communist Party office, and I saw Mr Bunting there. I used to go to the office when the communist newspaper was printed, and sometimes I would go from house to house delivering the papers myself. They would give me a couple of pennies, and I would use this to go the bioscope and buy something sweet.

In 1922, after the strike, the police came to our house in Simmonds Street, and turned everything upside down, looking for communist leaflets and books, anything that had to do with communism. On the wall there was a picture of the Soviet Union's sickle and hammer. One of the policemen tore it down from the wall and broke it over my dad's head. My dad was arrested and was released after ten days. My mother was glad that he came out, and she urged him to forget his communist ideas. He didn't listen to her, of course. So, as he was a communist, he was not able to get work after the strike as an engineer. So he became a tailor and was very prosperous in those years. He had a working place near the Carlton Hotel, which was right in the heart of Johannesburg. As we all grew up, my father decided to open up a fried fish and chip shop. The first shop, as far as I remember, was in Jeppestown, and the last shop before leaving South Africa was in Fordsburg.

AD Your mother was not happy that your father was in the Communist Party?

JG That's right. She begged him to leave it. But he didn't listen. One day, he read in the newspaper that Stalin would like to have engineers come to the Soviet Union and help the country to develop industrially. My dad began to talk about this with my mother. She was against it but he was stubborn. He told me that he would take me along. For me it was an adventure. I myself have never believed in communist ideas, even while I lived here.

So in 1931 we left South Africa for the Soviet Union. We sailed on a German boat from Laurenco Marques [now Maputo]. My dad bought me a camera there, and ever since I have gone around with a camera. Taking photographs became a hobby for me. We sailed around the coast of South Africa, stopping in Durban, Port Elizabeth and Cape Town to England. This was cheaper than passing through the Suez Canal. When we arrived in Durban we were travelling third class. But some black people had boarded the boat, and there was no place for them, so we were transferred to second class to make room for them. My father was very pleased with this luck. He saw it as a very good sign for us. He said: 'There you are Joe. Our travel to the Soviet Union has begun with a big bang.'

Initially, our visa was not granted by the Soviet Union. So we went to Lodz, in Poland, where my father had many relatives. My dad was always in communication with the Russian consulate in Berlin. At the end of a year the authorities gave us permission to enter the Soviet Union. We crossed the border into the Soviet Union at Negorilia around December 1932. While we were in Negorilia, my dad was invited to go into the captain's house. I was in the carriage waiting for my dad to come back. When he returned, I could see that he was very much disappointed. I asked him what was up. He didn't tell me why at that time but afterwards, when the train had left for Moscow, he told me that he had been searched, which was very humiliating for him. He had never before been searched. On the train he began to speak to some of the passengers—he knew a little Russian. He asked what it was like in Russia and how was Stalin doing. He had read in some of the Polish newspapers that Stalin was not well. The passengers kept quiet. They didn't want to answer, to speak with him, to have anything to do with him. He was a foreigner. My father couldn't understand this. I could not speak with them either, because I didn't speak Russian. I only spoke a little German.

We arrived in Moscow and went to live for a couple of days in the hotel where the Hotel Rossiya is now, right near the Kremlin on the slope from Red Square right down to the Moscow River. Afterwards—I don't know why—my dad was invited to live in one of those big buildings in which lived the elite, the big shots of the Communist Party who worked in the Kremlin. It was called the government house. We lived there for some time. But then the inhabitant of the flat told us that he couldn't keep us any longer. I don't know why. But I believe it might be because we had left some luggage in the baggage room of the hotel we had stayed in, and when we went back for it, we found there was plenty of lice! This may have been the reason we had to leave. I don't know if you should write about this or not!

After some time my dad was given a flat in a quickly made wooden building. We lived there for some years until my dad was arrested. My mother came for a couple of months in 1934, along with Michael and Aubrey. My brother Barney, the oldest, never came. But my mother didn't like it and left. She returned to South Africa, and Michael was going to go back to South Africa but stopped off in England and remained there.

AD When did you begin to feel that something was wrong in the Soviet Union?

JG The very first day. When we arrived in the Soviet Union things were bad, very bad indeed. My father had British pounds with him. In Moscow, there is a grocery store called Yeliseyev's, on Tverskaya Street. At that time, in the early 1930s, it was a store for foreigners, and it was called Torgsin—trading with foreigners. You could only buy products with foreign currency. We managed to live for a couple of months with my dad's British pounds. An interesting incident occurred. While I was waiting outside the store on Tverskaya Street, a gentleman came up to me and said something in Russian. I didn't understand him, as I didn't know Russian when we first came out to this country. He began to gesture with his fingers. He could see immediately that I was a foreigner. I was well dressed by comparison with most Russians, who were badly dressed in those days, and also, I was standing just outside Torgsin. He took me by the hand across the street, looked around and began to explain to me in Russian what he wanted. All the same, I couldn't understand. Then he waved at me and went away. I crossed the street where I was waiting for my dad. My dad came out, and I explained what had happened. Ah, these Russian people, my dad said. They want to buy foreign currency. The man wanted to buy foreign currency and give me roubles in exchange. But he dare not stand near the store. Even if I did want to exchange money, there might have been someone from the NKVD [precursor to the KGB] standing around, and he would have been arrested. Such were the years of the 1930s and 1940s. A nightmare. Those were the nightmare years.

AD Were most of your father's and your friends Russian or foreigners?

JG I, myself, was amongst English-speaking people most of the time. I used to go to the Anglo-American School. I studied there for about a year or maybe a little longer. Then it was closed down. The Soviet authorities said that it was not a school but a spy centre.

AD Do you remember any students or teachers at the Anglo-American school?

JG Yes, I do. There was a friend of mine, Norman Margolis, who was American. I don't know where he is at present. There were two friends of mine who now work for the English radio company; the programme is in English. One of them is Joe Adamoff, who was from England, and the other is Boris Belitsky, who was also from abroad. The three Boft sisters also went there. One of them, Violet, became a ballet dancer. Many of the teachers were foreigners. I remember that one was a black man from the United States, and one was an Australian.

AD Were the students at this school the children of foreign communists who had come to the Soviet Union?

JG I don't think that my friends were. But maybe some of them were. Actually, I wasn't interested in who was or was not a communist. For me, communism is nothing at all. My wife, by the way, was a communist!

AD Were you surprised when the school was shut down for allegedly being a spy centre?

JG Yes, I was. After this, there was no other choice but for me to go to work. I got a job in a very big automobile plant, named after Stalin. It was a very hard job. The people there liked me; we got along. My foreman, by the way, was a Scottish man who had been living in the Soviet Union for quite a while.

AD Was he a communist?

JG No, he was one of the people who came to the Soviet Union to help to develop the country and build a new socialist state.

AD When was your father arrested?

JG He was arrested in 1935 and sentenced to five years of hard labour in a place called Potma, about 1000 kilometres south of Moscow.

AD Did your father have any idea that he was going to be arrested?

JG Never.

AD Had your father become critical of what he had found here or disillusioned?

JG If he was, he kept any disappointments to himself. You dare not open your mouth in English.

AD Is this because people might think you were a spy?

JG Maybe so.

AD What were your feelings about the Soviet Union at that time?

JG I wouldn't say that I was very much pleased. I was very disappointed.

AD How old were you when you started to work?

JG I was about seventeen. But later I was sacked as an enemy of the people.

AD Did you have any idea that this would happen?

JG No.

AD Did you ever hear from your father or receive news about him?

JG Nothing at all. I know nothing at all about when or where he died or where he was buried.

AD Subsequently, though, you found out that your father had died?

JG We never found out anything at all. Nobody informed us at all.

AD But later you found out that your father had died?

JG No, nothing, no information at all. I came to the conclusion that he has died, that's all.

AD But you have never heard officially that he died?
JG No. We were informed by the officials what camp he was in—Potma—and that is all.
AD Then he could have lived for many years.
JG Maybe he is still alive for all I know. But of course, that is impossible! We never heard anything at all from him. Maybe he did write. I am sure that he did. But those letters were censored. I know personally that I when I was sent to the gulag I could not communicate with my wife at all. We had no rights to write or to receive letters.
AD This must have been very hard for you.
JG Yes. Very, very hard. I came out here for the adventure. Once I arrived here, I had no wish to go back. I had that kind of character. But I couldn't go back even if I had wanted to. When I came to this country, I had no passport, although I was British. But once I arrived I was called to the police station and informed that I should take a Soviet passport.

The Soviet officials asked me what my name was. I told them 'Glazer'. But the Russian 'a' is pronounced 'ah'. So they christened me Glazer, with a short 'ah'. Then they asked my first name, and I said Joseph. They couldn't get that at all. They called me Jusef. Then my patronymic became Genrichovitch.

I went to work at another factory. I was given a fifteen day test. The job that I was given was perfectly done. Then one day the foreman came up to me and told me that he had to dismiss me. I asked him why, as he was very much satisfied with the job that I had been doing. He said, 'I'm sorry. I can't keep you any longer.' Afterwards I found out that I was sacked because of my documents. When you start a job, you fill out a blank form with all your particulars, such as where you were born. These documents are checked by the NKVD. Once a foreigner is working in a factory, and his father was arrested, of course they couldn't keep him any longer in that factory. And that was the reason I was sacked. Then I went to another factory, filled out the same blank form with all my particulars, worked there for about ten days—then sacked. Wherever I went to, I was sacked. I had to live on something. Then, one day in 1939 I was passing by the trolley bus park. There was a notice on the board that they were in need of trainee trolley bus drivers. So I dropped in to the office, and told them that I would like to become a trainee. But the first thing I told the woman at the office was the truth. I told her that my dad was arrested, whereas before that I had not mentioned anything at all about my dad. But I told this woman that my father was arrested. She didn't say anything at all but accepted me, and I began to work. I finished the school as a pupil of driving a trolley bus. I worked at the trolley bus park for ten years, until 1949, when I was arrested myself.

AD Were you in the army during the war?

JG I was in Moscow during the war.

AD Did you fight in the army?

JG No. Never. I didn't fight in the army. I wasn't taken into the army.

AD Is that because you were a foreigner?

JG Most likely because I was a foreigner. During the war I was a trolley bus driver in a trolley bus park in Moscow. Life was very hard. All of our products were rationed. We received only 600 grams of bread. Once we received a ration card for bread, once we bought bread, a bit of the card was cut off. Now, 600 grams of bread when you have no salami or cheese or anything substantial to eat with it is not much. It was very difficult. You always went about hungry. On 20 November, my birthday, in 1941, a few months after the war broke out, I came to the trolley bus terminus and there was a café there for the conductors and drivers. I told the saleswoman who was working there that it was my birthday. She gave me a cup of tea and added an extra two teaspoons of sugar! To sweeten it a little for my birthday!

AD When did you meet your wife?

JG In 1947, in Sokolniki, one of the biggest parks in Moscow. But we daren't get married at first. We kept our relationship secret. I was a foreigner, and she was Russian. I was also a Russian citizen but born abroad.

AD Did you have any clue that you were going to be arrested?

JG Nothing at all. I had no idea at all. I didn't even believe that people were being arrested. I had heard of it but I didn't believe it.

AD You thought that things were better than in the 1930s?

JG Yes. Those years, in the 1940s, all you could read in the newspapers was how wonderful our country was. It was a country of wonders. There was everything about Stalin. Stalin's constitution, Stalin's five-year plan. Stalin was our father, Stalin was everything to us. But one day, at work, my conductor didn't appear. Nobody knew where he was. He disappeared—that's all. When I was arrested myself, I was taken to Butyrki jail. I had to sign a paper that I was given a ten-year sentence.

AD Did they give any reason as to why they were arresting you and sentencing you?

JG No, no. They never told me anything at all. I just had to sign this statement and received a ten-year sentence. My hand was shivering as I signed the document. I had no trial at all. It was a three-man jury, and they decided everything for you. I had no word at all. I couldn't defend myself.

I had no advocate to defend me. The officer then took me to a cell, opened the door of the cell and shoved me in.

AD Were you alone in the cell?

JG In the cell? About fifty people ran up to me and asked how many years I had been sentenced to. I said I didn't know exactly. They told me that I was sentenced to ten years because in that cell that was the sentence that everyone had received. There were 75 people living in that cell, and it wasn't a very big one. There were bunks and people were just squeezed into those bunks.

AD Were they all men?

JG Yes, only men. Then I heard somebody yell out my name. I turned around, and saw my conductor! Can you imagine!

AD Amazing!

JG My conductor was there, and he had also been given a sentence of ten years—for no reason at all. All those people in that cellar were innocent people. And what kind of people? Not rogues. Not bandits. Honest people. Professors, ballet dancers, authors—those are the kind of people who were there. And even in the camps, the gulag, the majority of the people there were intellectual people.

AD Intellectuals and foreigners?

JG No. I believe I was the only foreigner there. They were all Russians.

AD And the conductor? Was he seen as an intellectual?

JG No. They arrested anybody. They interrogated them, and the interrogator had to squeeze anything out of you. If not, if they couldn't squeeze anything out of you, then you were sent down to the cellar, you were not allowed to sleep for two days. Because in the evening, just when you should be sleeping, the door opens, the soldier comes in and says one letter: 'G'. I say Glazer. 'G' meant it concerned me. Then he took me to be interrogated at ten o'clock in the evening. And you are kept in the interrogator's office until six o'clock in the morning, when everyone wakes up. Then you are sent back into the cell. But I am not allowed to sleep. So all day long I can't close my eyes. The soldier is by the door, and there is a pigeonhole in the door. He opens up the pigeonhole, takes a look at you, and God forbid that you are sleeping, or even closing your eyes if he opens up that pigeonhole. Then, you are sent once more down to the cellar, where it is very cold, with a cold wind. It was terrible.

AD So they tortured you by denying you sleep.

JG Well, they didn't exactly torture me but they didn't allow me to sleep.

AD Yes, they denied you sleep.

JG When you come back to the interrogator after not sleeping 24 or 48 hours, you are glad to sign anything. And so I was given a ten-year sentence.

AD Did your wife know anything about where you were or what was happening?

JG She knew that I was arrested because they came at two o'clock in the morning. There was a knock at the door. They asked: 'Are you Glazer?'. I said, 'yes'. They said: 'We have a warrant for your arrest'. I said, 'There must be some mistake'. They said: 'We never make mistakes'. Of course, they began to search the flat. My wife was told to leave the flat. The flat was sealed. My wife returned. At that moment she was six months pregnant. You can imagine how she felt. Arresting an innocent man.

AD And then you went to a gulag?

JG Yes, they sent me to a gulag. I was interrogated for nine months, and then I was sent off to Karaganda.

AD How did you get there? Were you sent in a train?

JG By cattle train. We were packed in like herrings on bunks. But it was my luck that I was sent off to Karaganda and not to the Far East, where people were worse off. There were mosquitos there, they were cutting trees, people died by the thousands. Even in Karaganda, where I was sent, people died too, from poor nourishment, bad treatment, humiliation.

AD Humiliation?

JG Yes, humiliation. People were humiliated always.

AD How were they humiliated?

JG The guards would humiliate them. Coming out before work, after breakfast—if you can call it a breakfast!—you were sent off to work. Five people in one row. Before leaving the zone of the camp of the gulag, we were searched. We were taken outside the gates, where we waited for the rest of the brigade to come out. Then we were counted once more by the chief of the convoy, and then he shouted out, 'Forward, march'. A step to the right or a step to the left were counted as an attempted escape and you were liable to be shot. Forward march, and then we went to work. Of course working on these objects, on top of the buildings, when it was very cold was very, very hard. In the mornings, our daily ration of bread was 600 grams. You could do what you liked with it, breakfast or supper, whatever. That was our daily ration.

AD What about to drink?

JG They gave us a kind of porridge—if you can call it a porridge. It was just water. At this object where we were working, there was a cook who cooked for us. He was also a prisoner. But he was given very few products to cook with. It was all water. You eat water, drink water. We, the prisoners, used to joke that Karaganda—it is a very young town—was built on a sackful of oats.

AD Could you tell me about your life in the gulag? How many people were there, what was the daily life like, how did people survive, emotionally and physically?

JG When we arrived at this gulag, we were accommodated in barracks, with long corridors, and to the left and to the right were rooms for the brigades. Each brigade had its own room. In one brigade there were about thirty or forty people, living in a room about four metres by five metres. Early in the morning, at six o'clock, they woke us up, both winter and summer, in the rain, frost or cold. We were given our 'breakfast' and then sent off to work. Arriving at work, we had to work all day long till the sunset, because the guards and the convoy were frightened to take us out when it was dark. So from early morning till late at night, we were at work. It was very difficult of course, especially in the winter. You were working in open space, in the cold, and there was no place for us to hide ourselves from the rain and from the frost, especially in the winter. Of course, the same kind of liquid food was fed to us at lunch. We just had time to eat liquid food with no nourishment in it at all. Of course, there was no fruit! When the sun began to set we were taken back to the camps, and again once more, before entering the gates of the camps, we were searched to ensure that we did not bring any blades or knives along with us. We were then ready to be ourselves, alone. Of course, we all ran quickly. Those few who had received parcels from home ran to the kitchen to cook their food. I had nothing to do. I just had to eat that which was given to me, which was very, very little.

AD How was it that some people were able to receive parcels?

JG Very few people received parcels. How they managed to receive them, I don't know. We were not allowed, in general, to receive parcels or even letters. We were forbidden to receive letters. But somehow they did come through. That is the way we spent our lives all those years in the camps. Of course, the officers subjected us to humiliation. Once two persons escaped but were caught and were brought back to the camp. The whole day long we had to stand on our feet in the heat in the summertime. We weren't allowed to sit down. From early morning till late in the evening we had to stand with our hands behind our backs as punishment for those two who had tried to escape, so that we, in the future, should not think of escaping. They take great precautions to make sure that you shouldn't escape at all. They subjected us to anything they could think of.

There were many moments like that, of course. I, myself, was once led to the cellar, to the barrack of torture, let's call it. Down below in the cellar there was only a kind of bed made out of brick and lime, and you had to sleep on that bed with no pillow, nothing at all. The reason I was sent there was that the brigadier of our brigade began to beat people, he beat one of the foremen, and everyone of the brigade was sent down to this cell, individually. We were all alone, it was very cold down there, even though it was summer. We weren't fed at all. We were just a piece of wreckage when we were freed, just a piece of wreckage. We could hardly look at the light anymore, having been in the dark cellar. Things like that were everyday life for us. We couldn't do anything at all about it. We were punished for no reason at all. It was a pity. You look at these people, and who were they after all? Innocent people...intellectuals.

AD Were there also women in the same camp?

JG No. There were camps especially for women. In my camp there were only men.

AD So you were denied all contact of any sort with women?

JG That's right.

AD And there were no children or families there?

JG Children? There were no children. No families at all.

AD Did you make friends there? Did people talk to each other about their lives there or anything else?

JG Not really. Well, I had a friend there. He had been in China. There was a special settlement in China—Harbin—for Russians who lived there.[27] I became friends with him. He was in a very bad state. He was forever hungry. And he could hardly work. He was in bad health. And he wanted to commit suicide. I told him that he shouldn't do it because this had to end sometime, this suffering of ours. He, being in such a state, went up to the no man's land, the area between the fence, then barbed wire, and the camp itself. As he came up to the no man's land and the barbed wire, the soldier on guard on the tower told him to keep clear of the barbed wire. He didn't listen. The soldier on the tower shot him and killed him immediately. This man had been my friend.

AD When was that?

JG That was about 1952. Stalin died in 1953. After the death of Stalin things became easier for us.

AD What was your friend's name?

JG I don't remember.

AD Did he have a family?

JG Yes, he had a family but he also was deprived of any communication with his family, as we all were.

AD How long had you known him?

JG I knew him a little less than a year.

AD So, in a way, he did commit suicide, in that he went where he knew he would be shot.

JG Yes.

AD Was that unusual? Did other people do that?

JG No, that was unusual. We wanted to take him away after he was shot. It was a very cold day. He lay on the ground, just as he fell, with his feet tucked under him, and he froze. He was just a bit of frozen meat. But the guard on the tower didn't allow anybody to take him away. Then the officials came, and they allowed us to take him to a barrack. I don't know his fate after that. But he was buried.

At the camp people died by the hundreds. One time somebody got wind of a prisoner who had been buried naked. So they got together five prisoners—I was one of them—to go to the place where he was buried and dig out his body. He had been buried without a coffin. The soldiers had given us clothes to dress him, and then we were supposed to throw him back into the trench. We dug him out but I didn't do anything else because the whole thing was terrifying. It was horrible. I told the soldier I was not going to put any clothes on him. What was the point of that? To make us do that just for the sake of dressing him? Of course it was written back in the report that he was dressed.

AD So you didn't put clothes on him?

JG I didn't. I just couldn't do it. I helped to dig him out but I couldn't put clothes on him. I refused. He had to be cleaned first; all that mud had to be taken off. It was terrible.

AD Were the others prisoners able to dress him?

JG Yes. I suppose they were more tough than I was.

AD What do you think was the purpose of those camps?

JG Millions of people were arrested. They had to be accommodated somewhere. As I told you Karaganda was a new town built by the prisoners. At Karaganda there was not just one camp. There were many of them. And about thirty kilometres south of Karaganda was a place called Spassk.[28] There the conditions of the workers, the prisoners, were even worse than at our place. It all depended on the chief of the camp.

AD How did you find out about Spassk?

JG Journalists found out about it.

AD Did you find out about Spassk after you had been released?

JG Yes. But we already knew while we were Karaganda that we would not like to have been sent to Spassk. From time to time people were sent from one camp to another to make sure that you wouldn't get used to one of them or find a way to escape.

AD Were you moved at all?

JG Hardly. I was moved only once, from one camp to another, during the time I was in Karaganda. But I was afraid of being sent, of course, to Spassk.

AD What camp were you moved to?

JG I was moved from one camp in Karaganda to another in Karaganda. All around Karaganda there were many camps.

AD Did people ever talk about the situation or try to plan to escape?

JG Personally, no one ever came up to me and picked up that subject. But it was impossible to escape because these camps were surrounded by guards, barbed wire, no man's land. You daren't go up to the barbed wires. And in the evenings, projector lights lit up the place.

AD What about the toilet facilities? Were there latrines?

JG Oh no. Outside. There were no conveniences at all. You just went outside. You washed yourself in one big room, where they had washing boxes. And once a month you were taken to a bath, to a banya as they say in Russian, to the baths. The water wasn't very hot, just lukewarm, and somehow you had to wash yourself. But we were given clean clothes—more or less clean—after the bath. We had nothing of our own.

AD Nothing at all?

JG The only thing we had was pea jackets and hats. On our pea jackets we had a number written. We weren't Mr Glazer or Mr Petrov or anything like that. We were prisoner 3566 or another number. And you could not leave the camp without any number on your coat or your hat. You were given a piece of material, and you had to stitch it on to your coat or jacket—depending on what clothes you were wearing—with your number on it. We were prisoner number so and so, number this or that.

AD And you were prisoner number 3566?

JG Yes, that's right. The funny thing about it all is that it was not robots who created the gulag, but human beings, Russians, of flesh and blood. There you are. But as I was telling you, if they didn't arrest us, if they didn't send us off to camps, they would be arrested themselves. They were forced. Maybe he was a decent person, the interrogator. But what could he do? He had to find some kind of a reason to send you off to a camp. If not, he would be sent there himself.

AD What about your brother Aubrey? What happened to him during these years?

JG Aubrey was living in a terrible state. He was free but was evacuated out of Moscow, working day and night. Many people were evacuated out of

Moscow during the war because the German soldiers were approaching Moscow. He was with his wife. It was really difficult for them. But after the death of Stalin things became easier. Aubrey died about ten years ago.

AD Were you in contact with your brother Michael during these years?

JG Michael left in 1934. As he is not much of a writer, we lost all contact.

AD Did he know that his father had been picked up and sent to the gulag?

JG No. He didn't know that I was arrested either, until I got in contact with the English Red Cross. I wrote them a letter, and they told me I should get in touch with the Russian Red Cross. But they found my brother Michael in England and my brother Barney in South Africa. My brother Michael and I began to correspond with each other, although he is not much of a writer. He is a philatelist. I sent him Russian stamps, and he sent me British first day covers.

AD Do you feel that the terror of the 1940s differed from that of the 1930s? You said earlier, for instance, that you had heard that people were being sent to the gulag in the 1940s, but had not believed it.

JG In the 1930s, when people were arrested, they were denounced as enemies of the people. There was a very big propaganda campaign in the newspapers and the magazines. People read about it. Even the prosecutors said that we have to dig them out, arrest them and send them off to camps. I suppose you know that many famous communists, many famous generals were arrested and sent off to camps or they were even executed down below in the NKVD building, Lubyanka, in the centre of Moscow.

AD So did this change in the 1940s?

JG Yes. In the 1940s there was no such propaganda about enemies of the people. Not in the newspapers. Yet people were arrested by the thousands. Yet everybody kept quiet, though they knew about it. I didn't believe it. I believed in the newspaper propaganda. Everything was fine, everything was wonderful in our country.

AD Why do think there was no longer any open propaganda about enemies of the people in the 1940s?

JG You daren't say a word. You don't even say that American cars or even fountain pens were better than those in the Soviet Union. For that they found a reason to be arrested. When I was being interrogated, I noticed that my interrogator was writing with a ball point pen. We didn't have ball point pens in those years. I told him, you yourself are writing not with a Soviet pen but with an American pen. He came up to me and gave me a slap across the face and added to that a kick in the shin. I could hardly walk after that. But he didn't say anything after that. He kept quiet. He daren't say anything else after that.

AD How did you feel about life when you got out of the gulag?

JG I tried to forget that I ever was there. There was nothing I could think of that could make me glad. But I got a job again, things were a little better after the death of Stalin, so I got along nicely, came back to Moscow, lived with my family, everything was OK. In fact, I can't say that during my life in the Soviet Union or Russia, I was ever rich. I was neither rich nor poor. But I couldn't grumble. Grumbling won't help. And even during the time that I was interrogated, I have nothing against the interrogators, the soldiers in the camp, even Stalin. The only thing left for me to do is to live with my family. I love them and they love me. I am very happy to be with them. Of course I try not to remember those horrible, terrible days.

AD I am sorry that I made you remember them.

JG That's OK. It's your job. If I can do anything to help anybody, I will. Just for the sake of letting people know what it means to live in a communist state.

We have an organisation called the Association of Victims of Political Repression. In Podolsk there are 120 victims. October thirtieth is the day of victims of political repression. We get together near a monument, and there are speeches, and we may get a few roubles if there is any money.

I went back to Karaganda for a few days in November 1992. My wife and I visited a field at Spassk, about forty kilometres from Karaganda where there is a burial ground. Thousands of people were buried there but there is no memorial at all to those people. We went there with the journalist, Katya Kuznetsova. At one point—I didn't know they were filming—my wife came across a monument. It was for Estonians. She is Estonian, and she went up to it and put her arms around it. I started to cry.

AD Has a monument been built there for those who died in the gulag?

JG No, there is just an empty field even to this day. About five years ago, I went to the state Duma when Solzhenitsyn was speaking. I went up to him and began to speak with him in English, because he was living in America. I was excited to speak with him. I told him that I also was a victim of repression. He didn't want to speak with me in English, so I began speaking in Russian. I told him that I had been in Karaganda where political prisoners were just thrown in graves after they died. I asked him if he could possibly arrange for a monument where they are buried. He did not answer because there were people who seemed to be security guards seeing him off. So there was not enough time for him to answer.

Yeltsin stated that victims of repression should have the same rights as soldiers of World War Two. At first we did. But now we have nothing, and people have forgotten there were such things. Even Gennady Zyuganov, the head of the Communist Party, has said there were no political prisoners at all.[29] It is important that people do not forget that these things happened.

Notes

This interview was conducted as part of aproject funded by the British Academy. I am grateful to the Academy for its support.

1. Daria Merkusheva, 'Even Stalin couldn't scare off this expat', *Moscow Times*, 27 August 2001, p.1; 'A true English gentleman looks back on life in Stalin's camps', *Independent*, 29 August 2001; 'A Brit abroad', *Guardian*, 29 August 2001.
2. Application for naturalisation, Transvaal, 1908–9, TAB, CS 876, ref. 15531, and Application for letters of naturalisation, Cape Colony, 1907, KAB, CO 8613, ref. 22, both in National Archives of South Africa, Pretoria. My thanks to Ilma Brink for sending me copies of this material.
3. E. A. Mantzaris, 'Radical Community: the Yiddish-speaking branch of the International Socialist League, 1918–1920', in Belinda Bozzoli (ed.), *Class, Community and Conflict. South African perspectives* (Johannesburg, 1987), pp.160–76, esp. 164 and 172. Mantzaris, p.172, lists Glazer as a shopkeeper; but both earlier and later he is reported to be a tailor. See 'Trials under martial law', *Rand Daily Mail*, 16 March 1922, p.3.
4. On the Rand Revolt see, *inter alia*, W. M. MacMillan, 'The Truth about the Strike on the Rand,' *New Statesman*, xix, 474, 13 May 1922, pp.145–6; S. P. Bunting, 'The Rand Revolt: Causes and Effects', R. K. Cope Papers, A953/6a, Department of Historical Papers, University of the Witwatersrand Library; Edward Roux, '1922 and all that', *Trek*, 11 February 1944, p.12; Robert Davies, 'The 1922 Strike on the Rand. White labor and the political economy of South Africa', in Peter Gutkind, R. Cohen and J. Copans (eds), *African Labour History* (Beverly Hills and London, 1978), pp.80–108; Baruch Hirson, 'The General Strike of 1922', *Searchlight South Africa*, 3, 3 October 1993, pp.63–94; and Jeremy Krikler, 'The commandos: the army of white labour in South Africa', *Past and Present*, vol.163, no.3 (1999), pp.202–44.
5. 'Socialist arrested', *Star*, 13 March 1922, final stop-press edition, 4:30 pm, p.5.
6. Bunting, 'The Rand Revolt'. Despite white labour's prosperity relative to blacks, Bunting noted, p.4, that 'artisans from England often say they live no better in Africa than at "Home"; and many white miners are in some respects worse off than, until recently, their fellows in Wales, who at least escape the deadly South African "miner's phthisis", and are not so directly liable to be displaced by the advance of cheap non-european labor.' See Jack Simons and Ray Simons, *Class and Colour in South Africa, 1850–1950* (London, 1983), p.271, for a less sympathetic communist view.

7. Both the South African Mine Workers' Union, which adamantly refused to accept black members, and the South African Industrial Federation made it clear that their struggle was 'to protect the White race', 'to maintain a White standard of living', and 'to preserve White South Africa'. Indeed, the only banner seen at demonstrations on the Rand, evidently held up by white workers and their wives, bore the notorious slogan, 'Workers of the World Fight and Unite for a White S.A.'. This was not a CPSA slogan nor is there any evidence that communists supported it. See *Through the Red Revolt on the Rand. A pictorial review of events, January, February, March, 1922*, compiled from photographs taken by representatives of *The Star*, 1st and 2nd edns(Johannesburg, 1922).
8. Letter from F. to Ivon Jones, 16 March [1922], Russian State Archive of Socio-Political History (RGASPI), Moscow, 495.64.159.
9. 'Leaders arrested', *Rand Daily Mail*, 13 March 1922, p.3. Sidney Percival Bunting (1873–1936), born in London into a well-to-do Wesleyan family and educated at Magdalen College, Oxford, went to South Africa during the Anglo-Boer war, practised as a solicitor after the war and was gradually drawn into labour and left-wing politics. He joined the South African Labour Party in 1910 and later was a founding member of the War-on-War League, the International Socialist League and the CPSA. He was ousted from the CPSA in 1931 during the Class Against Class period.
10. 'Arrests in Johannesburg', *Rand Daily Mail*, 14 March 1922, 4; 'Trials under martial law', *Rand Daily Mail*, 16 March 1922, p.3.
11. S. P. Bunting, *'Red Revolt'. The Rand Strike, January-March, 1922* (Johannesburg, 1922), pp.22–3; Norman Herd, *1922. The revolt on the Rand* (Johannesburg, 1966), pp.47–8; Simons and Simons, *Class and Colour*, pp.294–6.
12. 'Trials under martial law'; 'Sentences: H. Glazer and 47 others', SAB, GG, 1725, ref. 51/6316, National Archives of South Africa, Pretoria. My thanks to Ilma Brink for sending me copies of this material.
13. 'Immigrants of the wrong sort…our human imports from Russia', *Rand Daily Mail*, 16 March 1922, p.3.
14. Simons and Simons, *Class and Colour*, pp.252–5, 271–99, 303; Herd, *1922*, pp.19–20.
15. Only a few communists were actively involved, and non-communist Afrikaners bore the brunt of the government's wrath after the strike. S. P. Bunting, *'Red Revolt'*, pp.32–3; Sheridan Johns, *Raising the Red Flag. The International Socialist League and the Communist Party of South Africa, 1914–1932* (Bellville, 1995), pp.139–43.
16. Simons and Simons, *Class and Colour*; Johns, *Red Flag*; Allison Drew, *Discordant Comrades. Identities and loyalties on the South African left* (Aldershot, 2000).
17. Drew, *Discordant Comrades*, pp.146–51. The three South African communists arrested in the late 1930s were Lazar Bach and the brothers Maurice and Paul Richter; all three died during their imprisonment.
18. Drew, *Discordant Comrades*, p.142.
19. Bernard Sachs, *Multitude of Dreams. A semi-autobiographical study* (Johannesburg, 1949), p.90.

20. Merkusheva, 'Even Stalin couldn't scare off this expat'. Aubrey remained in the Soviet Union and later became a taxi driver. See 'The happy grin on the face of Comrade Cabby', *Daily Mirror*, 3 December 1966, p.9. Barney, the eldest son, did not make the journey and remained in South Africa.
21. Aleksandr Solzhenitsyn was a prisoner at Karaganda from 1945 to 1953 and upon release was exiled for another three years. His novel, *One Day in the Life of Ivan Denisovich*, was first published in the literary journal *Novy Mir* (*New World*) in November 1962 with the agreement of Khrushchev.
22. Merkusheva, 'Even Stalin couldn't scare off this expat'.
23. Quoted in Susan Sachs, 'A new message but Russian's communist candidate can't escape past', *Newsday*, 4 June 1996, A07.
24. Quoted in Alan Philips, '"New" Russians find a soft spot for man of steel', *Daily Telegraph*, 8 March 1996, p.19. See also David Hoffman, 'Ex-foot soldier Zyuganov vies to lead Russia: communist leader's past one of rigid party loyalty', *Washington Post*, 2 June 1996, A01 and Jonathan Steele, 'Russia's red conservatives', *Guardian*, T24.
25. Amelia Gentleman, 'Forgotten ghosts of the gulag', *Observer*, 14 January 2001.
26. 'The singing fool' was produced in 1928.
27. The Russian community in Harbin grew with Russia's expansion of the Siberian railway into northeast China, especially after 1896. Harbin became the centre for this operation, although Russian influence there declined after its defeat in the Russo-Japanese War of 1904–5. Russians also emigrated to Harbin following the Russian revolution. Harbin was an influential milieu in the development of Marxist ideas in China and later became a centre of revolutionary and anti-imperialist struggle. After the Chinese revolution, Russian priests in Harbin were turned over to the Soviet authorities and imprisoned in the gulag.
28. Spassk-Dalniy was a centre for the construction and defense industries. As a prisoner at Karaganda, near Spaask, Aleksandr Solzhenitsyn helped to construct one of Spassk's major cement plants.
29. On Zyuganov's views of the gulag, see Sachs, 'A new message but Russian's communist candidate can't escape past'; Philips, '"New" Russians find a soft spot for man of steel'; and David Hoffman, 'Once a Loyal Party Soldier, Zyuganov Vies to Lead Russia', *Washington Post Foreign Service*, Sunday, 2 June 1996, A01.

The Historical Significance of the Russian Revolution
A roundtable discussion

Chaired by Francis King, with Edward Acton, Monty Johnstone, Boris Kagarlitsky and Hillel Ticktin

Francis King: On one famous occasion either Mao Zedong or Zhou Enlai (accounts vary) was asked about the historical significance of the French Revolution, and replied, 'It's too early to tell'. Nonetheless, the historical significance of the Russian Revolution of the early twentieth century is a question which begs to be addressed. At the time, the leaders and theoreticians of the Marxist groups in Russia had a ready-made schema for explaining the historical significance of revolutions, into which they tried to fit the events taking place around them. For the victorious Bolsheviks, a certain definite view of the revolution was an essential factor in legitimising their assumption of power in October 1917. It was not a purely Russian event, but marked the beginning of a historic global transition from capitalism to socialism and communism. For the Mensheviks, the position was less clear—their conception of Marxism precluded any possibility of a genuinely socialist revolution in Russia at that time, but nor could events in Russia after October 1917 be easily fitted into the schema of the bourgeois-democratic revolution.

Outside Russia's Marxist circles, other thinkers tried to make historical sense of events at the time. In 1918 the Russian liberal P. B. Struve, for example, described the revolution as an expression of 'national bankruptcy' and 'the fall of the Russian nation'.

Although only the Bolsheviks claimed any universal significance for the revolution, while their opponents tended to explain it more in terms of domestic factors, there was nonetheless a general view that these were events of world-historic importance.

Against the predictions of many observers at the time, the Soviet regime was able to consolidate itself. The spread of communist rule after 1945 seemed to confirm the Soviet view of the international significance of 1917, however much this view might have differed from Lenin's original conception. There was a general assumption that the process was all but irreversible, and this seemed to underpin much of Western foreign policy during the cold war. However, 1989–91 demonstrated that there was nothing irreversible about communist party rule, or the socio-economic system it brought with it. The collapse obliges us to rethink our views on the Russian Revolution. It would be hard to overestimate its importance in shaping twentieth century world history—but how, why and in what ways it shaped that history remains a contentious issue.

The first question I would like to raise, then, is this: how should we now regard the historical significance of the Russian Revolution? Was it the beginning of a (temporarily interrupted) worldwide process of replacing capitalism by socialism? Was it simply an extreme manifestation of an economic and political crisis experienced by many countries in the early stages of the process of modernisation? Or was it a peculiarly Russian event—a specific crisis of the Russian Empire, given a kind of millennial and universal significance by supporters and opponents alike?

Boris Kagarlitsky: There is no doubt that 1917 marked a new stage of a historic process. Whether it will after all lead to the replacement of capitalism by socialism is a different question because the collapse of civilisation and the end of humanity may be at least as likely (if not more likely) as an outcome. As Marx pointed out in the *Communist Manifesto* one possible outcome of class struggle may be the destruction of all rival classes together.

The process of bourgeois transformation took a few centuries and a lot of failed bourgeois revolutions (starting in the Czech lands and in Italy in the fifteenth century). In that sense the revolution in Russia can be seen as a failed revolution which nevertheless marked an important historic step in a struggle which started earlier and will not end after 1989 just because class struggle has objective reasons to exist. However there is another way to see this. Did the Russian Revolution actually fail? Is the process over?

The French Revolution didn't end in 1799 or even in 1814, its political impulse continued well into the mid-nineteenth century and only after 1870 can we speak about its final results. The English Revolution was more or less over only after 1688. I think what we now see is the stage of restoration in the revolutionary process which started in 1917 and still is not over. The next stage from the point of view of historical logic is the Glorious Revolution of Russian socialism.

Hillel Ticktin: I would divide the question of the historic significance of the October Revolution in two parts. In the first instance, it changed the epoch and hence history for ever. It overthrew the capitalist system in a part of the world, caused Russia to withdraw from the world market and from an imperialist military alliance, gave hope to millions that it could be overthrown and terrified the capitalist class for the same reason. It thereby permanently changed the class relations between capitalist and worker, between imperialist overlord and colonial subject and between all oppressors and exploiters and the oppressed and exploited. It thus both objectively and potentially weakened the mechanisms and forms of imperalist and capitalist control. Even the subsequent Stalinist counter-revolution could not alter what had happened. The intention, of course, was to assist the socialist revolution in the rest of the world since socialism in one country was and is a nonsense and they nearly succeeded. The fact that Europe did not go socialist is an historical accident. After the initial revolution in Germany in 1918, a socialist revolution could not be ruled out. That initial revolutionary period from 1917 to 1923 changed the world. In no sense can it be seen as a peculiarly Russian event, not least because practically every country of Europe experienced some level of support for the Russian Revolution and important countries had either insurrections or general strikes.

The second aspect of the October Revolution concerns the exact changes in the part of the world formerly occupied by the Tsarist Russian Empire. There the original October Revolution was effectively overthrown by the Stalinists, or, more correctly, by a new ruling group who replaced the old Bolsheviks who were exiled, imprisoned, killed or purged, except for a few who followed Stalin. History was rolled back but not to the Tsarist Empire, which could never be resuscitated. The 'Soviet Union' ceased to be a country where there were real 'Soviets' even in the diluted form down to 1923. It became a system so horrific in its atomisation and mass terrorisation that it was unique in these aspects alone. No aspect of the revolution or of socialism was permitted to exist except in its nominal form. Nonetheless, it is clear that while it was the antithesis of socialism itself, that antithesis only existed in order to destroy socialism.

The effect of the revolution was to turn the epoch into an epoch transitional to socialism but the intervention first of the social democrats and then Stalinism has prevented that transition proceeding on the ground. The modern forms of capitalism—the welfare state, semi-full employment, state control, are all part of the evolution of a declining capitalism but the transitional aspect has pushed these aspects much further than they would have gone without the revolution.

The overthrow of capitalism threw finance capital into a crisis from which it cannot recover. For the first time a country repudiated its debts in their entirety. France was knocked out as a finance capitalist country and Germany also lost out. Britain was too big an imperial power to lose in the same way and it had not invested to the same degree. The instability of France and Germany was, therefore, increased or rather the power of the ruling class in both those countries was reduced. It altered the basic nature of the ruling class in both those countries. At one and the same time, it reinforced the role of Great Britain and the United States, while compelling the ruling class of those countries to find an alternative means of control over the working class.

The revolution ushered in a period of permanent wars and revolutions. Under Stalinism that took the form of Stalinist wars, Stalinist-type liberation struggles and the war with fascism. That period is now over, we can now anticipate that we will return to the situation as it was after the revolution, with the difference of course that there is no revolution.

Francis: The responses of Hillel and Boris so far implicitly raise another important question: how many revolutions are we talking about here? Is a revolution first and foremost an event, or a process? If we regard revolution as a process, then October 1917 is simply an episode in that process. I would argue that the Russian Revolution was a process. It started around 1905, and was not completed, in the sense of a new social order having emerged in a more-or-less stable form, until the mid-1930s. In this view, 1917 represents the high point of that process, with two decisive events (February and October), but not two separate revolutions. The idea of two revolutions within 8 months, it seems to me, allowed the Bolsheviks to bring their practice into line with Russian Marxist orthodoxy (first the bourgeois-democratic revolution, then the proletarian one), but makes little historical sense. Nonetheless, if we talk about a process, there is the problem of when it begins and ends. In Hillel's presentation, it is rather short—by the end of 1923 a Stalinist counterrevolution was well underway. Boris seems to have a much longer perspective—raising the question of whether the revolution is over yet. The problem I have with the thesis of the Stalinist counterrevolution is that I cannot see when it began. Most of the monstrosities of high Stalinism—an all-powerful and arbitrary secret police, show trials, extra-judicial murder and incarceration of political opponents, hostage-taking, labour camps, no real rights for workers or peasants, and a callous disregard for human suffering—had their precedents in the practice of 1918–1923. At the same time, however, a new social and economic order was being formed, which is one of the functions of a revolution. That order almost certainly did not resemble the dreams of the men and women of 1917—but when has a revolution ever produced the society desired by the revolutionaries?

Monty Johnstone: Despite the communist implosions of recent years, the Russian Revolutions are certainly 'events of world-historic significance'. The October Revolution in particular inspired a formidable international revolutionary socialist movement, as well as exercising a powerful influence on and providing subsequent assistance to national liberation movements throughout the third world. It was the product of a deep economic, social and political crisis dating back to the previous century. It took two-and-a-half years of the First World War for all these critical elements to be exacerbated to the point of revolutionary explosion. Lenin said in May 1917: 'But for the war, Russia could have gone on living for years and decades without a revolution against the capitalists. The war has made that objectively impossible.'

Lenin believed by the autumn of 1917 that, internationally, 'a great turning point is at hand…We are on the threshold of a world proletarian revolution.' It was above all this conviction that led Lenin to abandon the previous Bolshevik belief that backward peasant Russia was unsuited to a socialist revolution. History shows that the Bolshevik decision to seize power in October 1917 was based on false expectations of successful revolutions in the West. In Russia itself the Bolsheviks had strong support from the workers above all in the industrial towns, but in the country as a whole (80 per cent peasant) they obtained only 24 per cent of the votes in the elections to the Constituent Assembly held in the weeks after the Bolsheviks had taken power and dissolved by them after its first meeting.

Under such conditions Lenin and the Bolsheviks judged that to keep in power introducing widespread socialist measures they had to apply coercive measures against other Soviet parties, which were effectively banned after 1921–2. Voices were raised against such measures at the time not only by Mensheviks like Martov but also by a number of members of the Bolshevik leadership predicting undesirable consequences. In trying to establish socialism in a backward country with only minority support there began already under Lenin to be enforced restrictions on democracy which were later to expand into Stalinism.

The collapse of communist party rule in the Soviet Union and Eastern Europe naturally undermined an 'unswerving' belief in 'world history' producing a 'historic global transition from capitalism to socialism.' The idea that the implosion, of which we are witnessing the shifting, prolonged and confused effects, is simply an interruption of some teleological process is a product of fideism rather than Marxism. The perspectives for these countries for many years ahead will only be able to be assessed by Marxists and non-Marxists alike through empirical observation and scientific analysis.

If this yields empirically grounded reasons for accepting the potential advantages of socialism over capitalist exploitation and globalisation, I for one will work for the former, eschewing Fukuyama's 'end of history' thesis.

Hillel: Francis made two points. One was that the revolution is a process. That is of course true. The traditional Marxist usage of revolution refers to a process in which one class is replaced by another. A coup does not replace one class by another. It is now standard, in the new right-wing orthodoxy of Russia, to call the October Revolution a coup, patently in order to obscure the very change in classes that the Bolsheviks did attempt to bring about. At any rate, if the point is that the revolution is in process today, I think that is true and of course my contribution was arguing that very point but in a global context, rather than in a Russian context. On the question of the difference between the Lenin-Trotsky period and the Stalinist period, Francis seems to use limited criteria. We can look at the aims: Under Lenin-Trotsky it is world revolution or at the very least a European revolution commencing in Germany, assisted by the USSR. Under Stalin it is socialism in one country, which is a theoretical nonsense, unless one understands it to mean an end to revolution and the nationalist building up of Russia. We can look at the socio-economic policies: Under Lenin-Trotsky, the Bolsheviks oppose the emergence of a separate privileged layer. Under Stalin it is welcomed, extended and becomes the dominant force in the economy. In foreign policy, the Bolsheviks are primarily interested in extending the world revolution, whereas under Stalin the Comintern is reduced to an agency of the Soviet Union and the communist parties become instruments of Soviet foreign policy, controlled and utilized by the NKVD. The argument that the Bolsheviks built up an all powerful secret police and did the same things, at least in principle, as Stalin is simply untrue. During war time many things have been done and have to be done to preserve the particular army involved. Usually bourgeois historiography ignores the real crimes committed by the generals in the First World War. We know some of them today.

One could put the reduction in civil rights under Lenin-Trotsky on a scale comparable to what happened in the West whereas what happened under Stalin was unique in world history. Most of us would condemn the world war itself as a monstrous imperialist act in which millions were sacrificed for the greater glory of the ruling class of different countries. The seven million killed in the civil war died because the West supported, encouraged and ensured that there was a civil war. Then too we should note that the histories of the civil war ignore the crimes committed by the right. The 70,000 Jews killed in pogroms in the time of the Civil War were almost all killed by the Whites. The argument for simple continuity between Lenin and Stalin has very little going for it.

Francis: My argument that there was continuity between Lenin and Stalin's rules does not mean that I regard their regimes as identical. That would be impossible—they ruled in different contexts, in different stages of the revolutionary process. But continuity there surely was—the Bolshevik regime of 1918 evolved into the Bolshevik regime of 1923, of 1928, of 1933, and so on, with the active consent of the overwhelming bulk of the party at all times. All the various 'oppositions' of the 1920s and early 1930s were pitiful affairs in terms of numbers and rank-and-file support. Almost all the tools and techniques which made Stalinism possible—both material and ideological—had been created before 1923. Nor were these measures purely temporary expedients of the civil war. It was not until 1921, after the war was won that the last remaining opposition parties in the soviets were finally liquidated, all factions within the Bolshevik party were banned, and the Cheka and GPU started to get involved in dealing with dissenters within the party itself. Stalinism seems a perfectly logical outcome to this style of rule.

I like Boris's notion that a revolutionary process has a kind of inner logic operating largely independently of the programmes and desires of the revolutionaries (and counterrevolutionaries) themselves. The danger, though, if we take this idea too far, is that we can end up like a bunch of generals planning how to fight the last war—Russian revolutionaries thought in terms of France, most twentieth-century revolutionaries have thought in terms of Russia, Che Guevara tried to reenact the Cuban Revolution in Africa and Bolivia, and so on. In relation to Russia—where is it now? Can 1991 be seen as part of a century-long revolutionary cycle, or should those events be seen as part of a new, largely separate cycle? Does the idea of revolutionary cycles have any use as a guide to predicting events, or is its main value in analysing events which have already happened?

Boris: The point made by Francis about the concept of revolutionary cycles being a poor guide for the future is right. But this is the problem of history in general. We need to learn and understand history to predict the future but basing our predictions on past experience is wrong. This sounds like a paradox but this is exactly how life is. I think that there is a logic in history there are certain laws and in that sense Hegelian-Marxist tradition is really very powerful. But that helps us to understand the stage we are in, not the scenario for concrete developments.

Edward Acton: I would like to join the discussion by addressing three of the interesting issues developed thus far by Francis, Hillel, Boris and Monty.

First: 1917, as Hillel rightly stresses, witnessed both political and social revolution, a shift in power between different classes more dramatic and abrupt than anywhere else in Europe. But the sequel to the October Revolution and the civil war which followed saw the crystallisation of a state which achieved an unprecedented level of autonomy from all social forces outside itself. Just when committed Marxists secured state power for the first time, Marx's central insight about the relationship between state and society ceased, for the first time, to be valid.

Second: the Soviet Revolution/experiment more broadly defined. In assessing its impact on the wider historical process, we must acknowledge the downside.

(1) It ensured that socialism in general and radical socialism in particular became identified with the policies and interests of one country: outside the USSR, socialists now found it desperately difficult to harmonise the language of social transformation with the language of nation and patriotism. The catastrophic effect was to enable the right, which had forfeited its hold on that language in 1917/18, to recapture it across much of Europe and beyond.

(2) Socialism and the socialist vision became identified with a regime and a social order which was a travesty of that vision. In choosing the fallen Russian Empire as the setting in which to put key components of socialism to the test, humanity chose about the most inhospitable conceivable political, social, economic, cultural, military and ideological context possible. And—surprise, surprise—the product was tragedy.

Third: The Fukuyamas and free marketeers dancing on the grave of the USSR may, in time, rue the day. The demand for collective control of all forms of power which underlay the Russian Revolution of 1917 was not unique to Russia nor was its fate bound up with that of the USSR. Outside the USSR collective action made vast strides in the course of the twentieth century. The removal of the incubus of association with the Soviet system, and that ghastly masquerade of a 'planned' economy, clears the way for a resurgence in optimism about conscious, non-market collective choice.

Monty: Francis's remarks about revolution lack any consideration of class. Lenin in April 1917 pertinently referred to 'the transfer of state power from one class to another class' as 'the first, the principal, the basic sign of a revolution.' The 'dress rehearsal' of 1905 did not take political power out of the hands of the Tsar and the feudal landed nobility. The revolution of February 1917 did do that and allowed dual power to be exercised for some months by the bourgeoisie and the workers' and soldiers' soviets. The economy however remained in capitalist and landlord ownership. It took the October Revolution to complete the bourgeois-democratic revolution by giving the land to the peasants seen as a 'by-product' of a 'proletarian-socialist revolution.' Although there is considerable room for debate as to which class(es) or caste(s) exercised state power after October 1917, there can be no dispute that the former ruling classes lost it. I do not see why Francis claims that two revolutions in 8 months (February and October) 'makes little historical sense'.

Francis says that all the 'monstrosities of high Stalinism ... had their precedents in the practice of 1918–1923'. This fails to recognise that such reprehensible phenomena were much more limited in this earlier period and existed then alongside real, if limited, elements of working class and peasant democracy.

Francis: Monty reproaches me for ignoring class factors. I accept that a genuine social and political revolution, like the one in Russia, involves a transfer of economic and political power from one or more classes or castes to another class, caste, or set of them. But I would argue that the new class relations only become apparent once the chaos of the main revolutionary upsurge has subsided. Prior to 1917, political and economic power was exercised by a combination of the Tsarist bureaucracy, the landowners, and the capitalists. By the early 1920s, it was being exercised by a party-state-Red Army bureaucracy, with only the peasants able to enjoy any degree of economic independence. This was the unprecedentedly autonomous state to which Edward refers. It is hard to speak of any group or class 'exercising power' in the chaos of the intervening period. Neither the bourgeoisie as a class, nor its political representatives were able to exert any effective control between February and October 1917. They tried, but failed hopelessly in the chaos of war and revolution. Similarly, I cannot see that the working class enjoyed any real 'power' after October 1917—a period characterised by the rapid disappearance of labour movement independence, the administrative suppression of other soviet (that is—working-class) parties, and a catastrophic decline in the working class itself. Or am I missing something?

Monty: I agree with Boris that there is a logic in history with the operation of certain laws. Applied to the Russian Revolution(s) this recognises that there were deep-seated objective phenomena acting within the old society without which neither Tsarism nor Kerensky would have been successfully overthrown. But did this logic necessarily have to result in the replacement of the old order by a Bolshevik regime? Were there not other alternatives which might have succeeded? Surely there was also a strong subjective element above all in the politics, personality and leadership capacity of Lenin. Even Trotsky, not prone to underestimate his own historical significance, said that without Lenin there would have been no successful October Revolution. The question of the actual scope of relevant historical laws and the respective weighting and interaction to be accorded to objective and subjective phenomena in studying the historical process is a crucial but extremely difficult one. There is always the danger of concluding in retrospect that something was inevitable because it happened—a practice from which the 'Hegelian-Marxist tradition' is sadly not exempt. In its worst form it appears as what Trotsky called 'the worship of the accomplished fact.' Hillel sees the fact that Europe did not follow Russia in carrying out a socialist revolution as 'an historical accident', for which he blames the Social Democrats (and later Stalinism). This seems to me a highly dubious proposition. By the Third Comintern Congress in 1921 Lenin was recognising that the major factor holding back the spread of revolution in Europe was the fact that the majority of the working class was following the Social Democrats rather than the Communists. There was nothing accidental about this. It was an objective factor with deep-seated historical causes present also today. Events like the 'Hands Off Russia' movement and the general strikes in Western Europe cited by Hillel should be clearly distinguished from a desire to follow the Moscow road of revolution.

Francis: At this stage I would like to raise a historiographical question—have historians tended to ignore the non-Russian aspects of the Russian Revolution? Have we concentrated too much on the all-Russian parties and movements and their political and economic struggles? In Great Russia itself, the revolutionary period was primarily about social and class struggles—workers against capitalists, peasants against landowners, soldiers against officers, all against the government etc., etc. Outside the ethnically Russian areas, there was a strong national element as well, which was able to predominate in Finland, Poland and the Baltic states, but was crushed elsewhere by the combined weight of Reds and Whites. For the ethnic Great Russians outside Great Russia itself, the main concern was generally with the all-Russian class and political struggles, whereas some native populations, however divided internally they may have been along class or social lines, tended to be united in seeing the fall of Tsarism as their opportunity to throw off the Russian yoke. The strength of the pro-independence forces in 1917 depended on several factors—for example, how Russified was the native population, how far were they integrated into all-Russian politics, and what, realistically, were the alternative imperial masters on offer. The gaze of the Russian revolutionaries before 1917 was always fixed firmly on the West. There are very few references in any of their works to such places as Turkestan, where there had been a massive uprising against Russian rule in 1916, and little evidence of any interest in those areas. But when we try to assess the historical experience of the Russian Revolution, is there not a good case for seeing it in some respects as a series of national revolutions each with their own internal dynamics? And if we are going to look at revolutions in terms of cycles, could we regard the attainment of independence by the union republics in 1991 as the completion of cycles begun in 1917, but then interrupted? Were the non-Russian national revolutions, in effect, defeated by the all-Russian imperial revolution?

Hillel: The question raised by Francis on the national question pinpoints an essential premise underlying the discussion. The Bolsheviks did not imagine when taking power in October 1917 that they would have to run the Russian Empire as an isolated non-socialist entity. Even Stalin rejected the concept of socialism in one country in 1917. Given that all attempts at revolution in the West failed, what conclusions can we draw?

(1) Monty has argued that the revolution of 1917 was based on a false premise: that there could be a revolution in the West. I think it is worth exploring this issue, even though I profoundly disagree with Monty. Lenin famously used the analogy of the chain broken at the weakest link. Was he right? If he was wrong, was he proved wrong by historical necessity or historical accident? In either case, and this is the point, what was the Communist Party to do, once they realised their predicament?

(2) Lenin's chain analogy brings out the integral world nature of capitalism, which is crucial to understanding the effects of the Russian Revolution. I think that we need another analogy to understand the ongoing irreversible changes made to capitalism. (I prefer that of a building with its foundations permanently undermined but which can go on being constructed for a period of time.)

(3) Were Lenin/Trotsky and the Bolshevik party correct to take power at that point? Today, in my view, we have to say that it was a gamble, but that not taking power at that time was also a gamble with profound counter-revolutionary consequences. The peace of Brest Litovsk was

another gamble, even though it might have looked like the least dangerous solution at the time. As I understand it, failure of the revolution in the West was accidental. Given other decisions by either side or other historical accidents, the revolution might have taken place. The same scenario is likely to repeat itself, hopefully not time and again, but any time battle is made between the working class and the ruling class. There is always the possibility that historical accident will overcome the working class.

(4) Should Lenin/Trotsky have remained in power after 1921, when it was clear that the German Revolution had either failed or at least paused? Should the Bolsheviks have taken the next train to Switzerland? Should Trotsky have taken power when he could have done so against Stalin? The reasons for history evolving in the way that it did are well known and no one could have foreseen the awful denouement in the Soviet Union itself. Today looking back we might conclude that almost anything else would have been better, but that is not history.

How far were the Bolsheviks justified in taking power without the support of the peasantry and of the population of the national republics from the Ukraine to Central Asia? That is the underlying question which has to be faced. The case of the Ukraine is clearest, where the Mensheviks had the majority of the working class, leaving the Bolsheviks with little indigenous support. In fact, Christian Rakovsky, as prime minister of the Ukraine, reversed the mistaken early Bolshevik policy and went for Ukrainisation. Support did develop but it was bound to be limited.

There can be no question but that the Communist Party invaded a series of national republics or countries and then imposed a regime transitional to what they hoped would be socialism. In that process, precisely because it was imposed, they committed a series of blunders, some of which were reversed in the early years but which Stalinism magnified and changed into a system which in some cases was similar to colonialism.

This again brings into focus Francis's point about the meaning of the dictatorship of the proletariat when there were few if any institutional means of workers participating in decision making. Without the latter, the concept, in the long run, must become mystical. The usual view rests on the measures taken, which were in the interests of the working class. I think we can argue that insofar as those measures were egalitarian and not in any way intended or used to support the personal interests of the ruling group, there was some measure of the proletarian dictatorship, even if by proxy, as it were. But such a form of the proletarian dictatorship cannot be sustained for any length of time.

We can also look at the process in another way: as Trotsky put it, after every revolution there is a counter-revolution. It does not go the whole way back, but it does lead to the defeat of leading revolutionaries. That is what happened in the USSR.

What came into being, therefore, was an historical accident, a system which was not a mode of production, a non-viable entity which thrashed this way and that until it finally brought itself to an end. In a sense, I am saying that whereas the revolutionaries of 1917–23 wanted to overthrow capitalism worldwide, the Stalinists would have preferred to have capitalism but settled for what was possible in the circumstances.

Boris: We are mixing two separate questions. The revolution in a multinational empire is a separate question. It is not directly linked to the question about about whether the Russian Revolution could have succeeded as a socialist one. Revolution was happenning anyhow and it had its internal momentum which brought the Bolsheviks to power as the most radical force within the revolutionary camp (like the Taborites in the Czech lands in the fifteenth century, the Independents in England in the seventeenth century or the Jacobins in France in the eighteenth). Even if the Bolsheviks were not confused about the perspectives of revolution in Germany that didn't change much in this respect. As for the multinational aspect of the revolution, there were different conflicts and struggles mixed in the same process. Look at the civil war in the Ukraine. There were many sides, not just Reds and Whites. Central Asia with its 'colonial revolution' is a separate story. As well as Georgia with its Menshevik-led revolution. This needs to be studied and, honestly, a really full history of the Russian 'imperial' revolution has yet to be written.

Monty: Francis has drawn attention to the importance of the non-Russian aspects of the Russian Revolution with their specific characteristics. It would be a mistake however to see them as 'a series of national revolutions' (how many?). In fact the main initial impetus for the October Revolution came from the centre and from the industrial areas pursuing similar objectives. Francis suggests that the attainment of independence by the Union Republics in 1991 'was a completion of cycles begun in 1917.' In fact it seems to me extremely hazardous to refer to the 'completion' of anything in the shambles of the last decade. And talk of 'all-Russian imperial revolution' is surely fanciful.

Francis seems to imply that it would have been a good thing if in the civil war the territories which were to form the USSR had been broken up. In my judgement this would have had tragic consequences either through its displacement by one or more military dictatorships and/or a relapse into primitive economic and social system(s), pogroms and arbitrariness. One can hardly imagine it would have provided a democratic alternative. The best chance for that (though no guarantee) would, I think, have been the formation already in November 1917 of a socialist coalition government which was canvassed at that time by the Left Mensheviks and Left SRs, the Railway Workers' trade union and a number of Bolshevik leaders, who publicly declared that 'a purely Bolshevik goverment can maintain itself only by political terror.' I wonder how Hillel feels about this? I seem to find myself between his pro- and Francis' anti Bolshevism!

Francis: On the question of socialism in one country raised by Hillel, I take the view expressed by the independent Marxist economist Bazarov in 1927 that it is an empirical question, not one of principle. Had the Soviet economic planners and administrators succeeded in developing economic mechanisms capable of outperforming capitalist mechanisms through more rational use of productive forces, then a) it would have been possible to proceed with the socialisation of the economy in an evolutionary way, without mass terror, and b) it would have provided the most powerful argument against capitalism imaginable. But we shall never know whether the work of the early planning economists could eventually have borne fruit, because from 1929 Stalin reintroduced siege economics into the USSR, where effective resource use, and workers' living standards, were all sacrificed in pursuit of gross output and state control at whatever cost.

As for the failed (?) German/European revolution, I have grave doubts about its hallowed place in Trotskyist historiography, because I cannot see how it would have helped Russia. Germany in 1918 was economically ruined. Whereas in 1917 in Russia, Lenin and the Bolsheviks appeared to many to offer the best prospects for peace, in Germany in 1919, the best guarantees of peace and reconstruction were Ebert, Scheidemann and the SPD. Had the Spartacist rising been a more serious affair, Germany would almost certainly have been consumed in civil war and have faced Allied intervention. Its economy would have collapsed still further. What, realistically, could it have shared with Soviet Russia, except the abject misery of its people and the revolutionary proclamations of its leaders?

Initially, the Bolsheviks' opponents made much of the claim that they were just a gang of adventurers with no interest in Russia, who were using it as a springboard for their international ambitions. The White forces in particular stressed the Jewish origins of many Bolshevik leaders, in order to suggest that the Bolshevik government was a non-Russian regime of occupation. But we know that that was not the case—from the outset, the Bolsheviks were very interested in ruling. They issued masses of decrees and undertook numerous reforms. Some of the decrees were more declamatory than legislative, some were rather naive, and others were perfectly serious. For the most part, they were aimed at addressing domestic problems. The international revolution loomed largest in their thinking in the early period when they had to address international problems—Brest-Litovsk, foreign intervention, and so forth. And from the outset, G. V. Chicherin was actively pursuing non-revolutionary diplomacy aimed at securing the position of Soviet Russia as a state. Did anyone among the Bolsheviks suggest surrendering power because of the non-arrival of the German or European revolution? After victory in the civil war, seeing off the intervention, and reconquering most of the old Tsarist empire? That would have run completely against the logic of everything they had worked so hard for. I quite agree with Boris, that the question of the national revolutions in the non-Russian areas is separate from the question of the chances for socialism in Great Russia. That is why I raised it as a separate historiographical question—are we missing something rather important when we look at 1917 if we concentrate solely on Great Russian politics?

I am a bit puzzled by Monty's advocacy of the socialist coalition government as a viable democratic alternative. The demand at the time was for 'a socialist coalition government until the convocation of the Constituent Assembly'. That is—it was proposed as a two-month stopgap. It was the Constituent Assembly which provided the best chances for democratic development, the peaceful secession of peripheral areas and so on. Once the Bolsheviks and Left SRs had wrecked the Assembly, it was clear that everything in Russia was to be decided by force. Events took on their own logic from there.

Hillel: Francis has raised the question of whether socialism in one country could have worked if not for Stalin. It is a very useful clarification of the question. Socialism, as I understand it, can only exist as a world system, like capitalism. In the case of a backward country, the situation, it seems to me, is much aggravated by its low standard of living and need to import the necessary capital equipment. The issue is not really a technical one, however. Let us assume the Bazarov/King case of the USSR without Stalin and Trotsky. It does not regard its rationale as that of assisting the move to socialism the world over but only that of building up the USSR itself, which it thinks is enough of a contribution to the cause of world socialism. Who is in power? Will it organise democratic elections among workers and peasants?

If it does so, the Bazarov faction will almost certainly lose out to a party representing the interests of market-peasants. If it organises elections among the workers only and perhaps introduces functioning Soviets, how will the workers and the towns relate to the countryside? Will the peasants really wait for the gradual improvements predicated on the Bazarov solution? Will the bureaucratic apparatus not demand its own share of the cake? Even in the best case, given the low standard of living, will not the intelligentsia and bureaucratic apparatus become gradually corrupted and demand not a controlled market but the full market? Can the market and plan really co-exist?

Francis rightly points out that the Lenin/Trotsky regime began constructing something new immediately and of course one does not need Bazarov to justify the concept of an isolated country in transition to socialism. Preobrazhensky argued exactly that case in one of his early books, *From NEP to Socialism*, saying that eventually the USSR would have to force the issue of socialism for the rest of the world, once it had attained a high level of productivity etc. (Trotsky did criticise him as having a tendency towards socialism in one country.) The question is the nature of the system that is being constructed in this period. The element of continuity between Lenin and Stalin lies in those elements which everyone condemns but which was probably necessary for the survival of the early regime. Put positively: without Soviets, without genuine—not bourgeois and not Stalinist—democracy what is one constructing? The basic law of socialism rests on planning, properly defined as the regulation of the economy by the associated producers themselves. Clearly this has never existed. In the early period, there were aspects and vestiges of control from below, progressively abolished.

I did say that it was an accident of history that there was no socialist revolution in the West but I did not say that either social democracy or Stalinism are accidents. Their evolution is an interweaving of accident and necessity. The kind of accidents to which I was referring are much like those to which Monty himself refers, incorrect decision making, weak personalities or people unsuited to the tasks etc. I do not think that the German working class necessarily had to go over to the social democrats or remain with them forever. There was no strong left wing party at the time of the German Revolution in November 1918 and that was at least partly the fault of the Spartacist leaders. Their assassination was not foreordained. Lenin's expulsion of Paul Levi was a disaster for the German party, etc., etc. Ruth Fischer, the German CP leader, considered the 1918–23 period as one of instability in which a revolution was possible. Clearly there is no way we can settle what is at least partly an empirical issue.

There is an inherent problem in separating accident from necessity in looking at a failed revolution, in that the issue is not a simple factual one. If the working class wants change, the ruling class is weak and cannot rule in the old way, whether there is a revolution will depend to a large extent on the revolutionary leadership and its form. Then too the situation can change from month to month. If we say, for instance, that the Spartacists were hopeless, Lenin had the wrong idea and the subsequent leaders were inferior does that mean that there was no chance of a revolution? Do we say that the masses were wedded to social democracy, whatever happened? That does seem to me an inevitabilist type of argument. In any case, a successful revolution will always remain an unexpected event. Strangely for Monty I am not far from the idea that a successful revolution has an element of accident in it.

A rather obvious accident, in the civil war, in this sense, occurred with Lenin's determined march on Poland and Tukhachevsky's defeat in 1920. (As it happens my father remembered the occasion because he was a youth at the time in Bialystok when the Red Army marched through and a Bialystok Soviet was set up. A cousin, on Trotsky's staff, came to dinner at the family flat.) If you look at the protocols of the relevant party conference in 1920 you will find that Lenin and Trotsky essentially blame Stalin for giving Tukhachevsky the wrong information and so orders. In effect Tukhachevsky believed that there would be an uprising in Warsaw and he had only to reach Warsaw to assist the revolutionaries. So he force marched his troops who arrived exhausted. He had then both the wrong strategy and a weakened army, so that it was not surprising that he lost. He may have lost anyway but there is a good chance that he would have succeeded. In spite of the reactionary Polish nationalists, there was some base among Polish workers but in any case the aim was to reach the border with Germany. Again we do not know whether that would have had the desired effect but it might have.

That kind of chance occurred a million times in the civil war. In this instance, it simply happened, if we believe the account, that Stalin was something of an optimist, if we are charitable, or an idiot if we are not.

Francis points out that Germany was ruined and could not therefore have done much to help Russia had there been a revolution there. His scenario of a prostrate country pushed back to the stone age by civil war or intervention may be correct. I would make these five points, nonetheless.

(1) The question of transfer of surplus in order to raise the national income: In this respect, even the use of skilled workers would have made a considerable difference, given the illiteracy of the population of the USSR. In reality, Germany could have made a very quick recovery as the Nazis unfortunately showed.

(2) The evolution of Germany towards Nazism would have been aborted and so provided more time for the development of the USSR.

(3) The revolutionary weight in the world could have grown to the point where the trade and investment boycotts may have been broken.

(4) The new German revolutionary leadership would probably have assumed control over the International, changed its Bolshevisation and prevented Stalin turning the International into a Stalinist agency. Other countries would probably have moved into its orbit.

(5) Crucially the effect of these results could have been enough to prevent the new Stalinist elite taking control.

I am not certain what Monty intends by asking what I would think of a coalition with the Left Mensheviks and Left SRs. Yes it does sound like a reasonable idea but would it have worked? In a sense, the evolution of Russia in 1917–18 was determined by outside events: the war and the intervention. I would have thought that either these two groups would have merged into the Bolshevik party or they would have broken with them, as happened.

The issue of the dissolution of the Constituent Assembly is critical because it did mean that the left effectively broke with democracy. (I find Luxemburg's comments rather feeble because she argued that Lenin ought not to have dissolved the Constituent Assembly until it showed its hand, at which point it was fine to remove it.) The legitimacy of the Bolshevik government after the dissolution of the Constituent Assembly rested on its claim to represent the working class but not the peasant owner/possessor of a plot. The context of the time, which is important, was one in which the UK, for instance, still excluded the majority of its population from voting.

Francis: Hillel has discerned the weakness in my 'Gosplan road to socialism' argument: the pioneering work on trying to devise mechanisms for a planned economy in the USSR in the 1920s, undertaken largely by democratically-minded ex-Menshevik economists, depended on the continued existence and goodwill of the Bolshevik dictatorship for support. When that support was withdrawn in favour of returning to a siege economy model of 'planning' after 1929, their work was abruptly aborted. But the question they were tackling—how to create a planned economic system capable of developing productive forces and increasing labour productivity more effectively than capitalism—should be a vital one for socialists, and it still has not been resolved today. According to the Marxian schema, less productive systems are ultimately displaced by more productive ones. You can have the most splendid revolutionary leadership imaginable, but if the post-revolutionary reconstruction cannot create an economic system that is more rational in its use of resources than the preceding system, then that revolution has failed. I cannot see that the scale of the revolution is crucial here—the technical problems would be much the same (although larger) on a global scale as on a national scale. Hillel raised the question of the coexistence of plan and market. The general perspective during NEP, of gradually replacing market mechanisms by planned ones as and when the latter had been created, seems to me to be the only sensible approach. Whether it was feasible in the specific conditions of the USSR in the 1920s is another matter, although the speed of economic restoration in the mid-1920s (when the Soviet economy was regulated, but not planned) was impressive by any standards.

Boris: The failure of the revolution in the West was not 'accidental' but was it absolutely inevitable? With Hillel's position I have one problem: it is very deterministic in the case of Russia but less so in the case of Western Europe. We have to put both sides of the story together. My view is that the outcome of the Russian Revolution actually strengthened the reformist forces in the West and weakened the revolutionary ones. But that was in the long run. I think that the Bolsheviks were wrong waiting for the revolution in 1918 but are we sure that there was no revolutionary potential in the 1920s? Are we sure that the influence of the Soviet Union on the labour movement and the revolutionary parties was so positive? In *The Dialectic of Hope* which I wrote 20 years ago I said that the outcome in the Soviet Union and Stalinism in particular pushed the Western labour movement towards social democratic positions. What were the impacts of Zinoviev's policies in the Comintern, and of the Soviet purges? How did the red terror affect the international perception of the Soviet Union? Don't forget, Russia had a civil war and Hillel's determinism is justified. But is it true that even minor changes of policies couldn't have made a difference?

Francis: Boris has raised some very important questions. Why do revolutions happen? They generally happen when an existing political and economic order is unable to adapt to accommodate the demands and interests of rising classes and social groups. If we try to list the social groups who were unhappy with Tsarism for one reason or another by 1917, they encompass virtually the entire population. If we add to that the fact that Russia was losing the war, it would have been remarkable indeed had the Tsarist state survived. And, as Boris has pointed out, the Bolsheviks were the most radical force around in a deteriorating and radicalising situation, like the Taborites, Independents and Jacobins before them. Did the same circumstances apply in the rest of Europe after the war? Not really. Once the nations of Central Europe had attained independence, their revolutionary fervour soon dissipated. Germany had a political revolution, but there was not the political or economic basis for a full-blown social revolution. And in Britain, there was never any serious threat to the existing order, because of the adaptability of its political system. But I don't see reformism primarily as a response to the existence of the USSR—it is surely more a reflection of the balance of social forces within Western countries themselves. In this respect, I take a view diametrically opposite to that of Hillel. Neither the success of Bolshevism in Russia, nor, even more so, the failure of its imitators in the West, were accidental. Each was conditioned by the specific circumstances prevailing in those respective areas.

Monty: Francis should not be 'puzzled' at my advocacy of a socialist coalition government as the best potentially viable democratic alternative for Russia in 1917. Lenin's calls from April to July, and again in September 1917 for an SR–Menshevik coalition government made it clear that he was envisaging this concept as a serious medium-term strategy, not just as a two-month 'stop gap' conceived briefly in September, until the convocation of the Constituent Assembly. Already in his *April Theses*, Lenin had called for the transfer of the entire power of the state to the soviets, and, for convoking the Constituent Assembly. In his article 'On Compromises' in early-mid September he strongly restated his proposals for a 'government of SRs and Mensheviks responsible to the Soviets', in which there would be a peaceful struggle of parties. The next month, he recognised the 'combined type' of Soviet power and Constituent Assembly. This position was reiterated in the Bolshevik leadership by Zinoviev and Kamenev on the eve of the October rising, after Lenin changed course. They foresaw the Bolsheviks in the Consitituent Assembly either as a strong opposition party, or 'in a ruling bloc with the Left-SRs, the non-party peasants and others'. That perspective corresponded broadly to that of a socialist coalition government based on the Constituent Assembly, for which there was real support in the country. Only with the dispersal of the Constituent Assembly did Lenin resolve in his fashion the objection that for the soviets to concentrate all power in their hands must prove incompatible with a commitment to a Constituent Assembly, elected by universal suffrage , and representing 'the sovereignty of the people' (as inscribed in the party programme).

Hillel asks whether Lenin and Trotsky should have remained in power after 1921 when it was clear that the German Revolution had failed. Whilst

I believe that a socialist coalition government would have been possible in October-November 1917, and even up to July 1918 (the Left SRs had been junior partners from December 1917 to March 1918), by 1921 a sharpened situation would have made that much more difficult.

On the 1920s controversy on the possibility of building socialism in one country, I agree with Francis (and Bazarov) that this should be regarded as an empirical question rather than a matter of principle. In fact, the debate on this issue was highly scholastic, with all the attributes of a pseudo-debate often taking the form of a battle of quotations. It contrasted with the real, and in essence largely unrelated (though often factionally aligned) controversies around economic planning and investment, living standards, international policy and crucial issues of democracy (though these debates became increasingly restricted). All the Bolsheviks, including Stalin on numerous occasions, stated their belief that the international spread of socialist revolution would provide by far the most desirable basis for solving the Soviet Union's problems. However, neither the example of the USSR, nor the work of the Comintern (before or after Lenin's death) was capable of bringing this about. Nonetheless, I see no reason to believe that, if the Trotskyist opposition to the concept of socialism in one country had secured a majority in the party, the prospect of avoiding the repressive degeneration of the Soviet state would have been much brighter. The basic cause for what went wrong is surely to be sought in the conditions in a backward country where power was seized, maintained and grossly expanded over time by an unaccountable minority.

I asked Hillel for his views on a socialist coalition government because I was interested to see if he would accept this as a viable alternative to the October 1917 overthrow which he concedes to have been a 'gamble'. I don't think his reply does the issue justice. No one can be sure, of course, that it would have succeeded. It was, however, increasingly favoured in the autumn of 1917 by the leftward-moving SRs and Mensheviks like Martov, who would never have merged with the Bolshevik party as Hillel suggests. It would have been the government of over 80 per cent of the population who voted for these parties in the CA elections in November 1917. Its realisation was prevented after the Bolsheviks took power partly by Lenin and Trotsky on one side, and by some right-wing Mensheviks on the other.

Hillel states that the Red Army's march into Poland in 1920 was 'a rather obvious accident in the civil war'. I disagree with this. Lenin made it clear to Clara Zetkin that more important than materiel deficiencies for this fiasco was 'our political miscalculation—the hope of a revolution in Poland'. In fact, 'the revolution in Poland on which we counted did not take place'. This belief was in my view no accident, but a deeply held conviction at that time on the part of Lenin and the majority of the Bolshevik and Comintern leadership. Lenin admitted to Zetkin that he had ignored Radek's correct prediction of disaster ahead, although the Polish revolutionary knew affairs outside Russia better than he did. This damaging experience disabused Lenin of such wishful thinking on revolutionary prospects as the success of October 1917 had encouraged in the previously hard-headed Bolshevik leader.

Hillel has in my view not made a convincing case as to why we should believe in the potential for Bolshevik-style revolutions outside Russia. If each of these situations deemed revolutionary or pre-revolutionary has been thwarted by one exceptional cause or another, must we conclude: what an extraordinary run of bad luck! Is it not more logical to conclude that there are deeper historical factors, referred to by Francis, why that type of revolution is not suited to developed capitalist countries like Britain? However, I am much more in agreement with Hillel than with Francis on most of the potential positive effects that he accords to a German socialist revolution…if only it had succeeded.

Francis: An argument I find attractive is this: just as capitalist economic mechanisms had developed over centuries before the bourgeoisie was ripe for political power, so the economic mechanisms required for socialism (thorough knowledge of economic processes, and the tools for effective conscious intervention and control) will need to have developed for some considerable time before the working class is able to dispense with bosses and run things in the interests of all. Destroying capitalist rule, or even capitalism, is the easy part. Putting something better in its place is where the real difficulties begin. That is why I find the planning debates of the 1920s so intriguing—it was the only period when these most fundamental questions of socialism were aired in the context of a practical attempt to resolve them, albeit somewhat technocratically and in the context of a tightening dictatorship. The planning economists did not find the answers, but they certainly found many of the questions.

Hillel: I agree with Francis that we still need a socialist plan. Stalinist so-called planning only took us backwards and I also agree that any shift to socialism will involve a gradual move away from the market to planning. Where it seems we do not agree, is that he ignores the socio-economic or class nature of the Stalinist rulers of the USSR after 1925 or so. I am not defining them as a a class but they nonetheless extracted a surplus product from the workers. This social group had its own interests and hence the policies adopted in the middle to late twenties down to the present have emanated from them. It, therefore, follows that it was not the Bolsheviks who stopped Bazarov but that group. In any case, most of the old Bolsheviks had either been killed or belonged to the left opposition.

I also think that Francis assumes that there are no class interests involved in the market and hence a shift to planning will occur painlessly. How does one have a market, when the proletariat is in power? Will the workers run the market enterprises? If not, will the workers not demand wages and conditions such that the firm makes a loss, so causing conflict with the managers or capitalists? Will the state not support workers' strikes? In other words, there is an automatic conflict between the exploitation of the worker within a market, his reduction to an abstract labour, and the rule of the worker. These are the elementary questions to which there never has been an answer but which indicate how fraught such a transition must be. It is also one more reason why an isolated country is unlikely to make such a transition.

In reply to Monty on socialism on one country, it seems to me that the issue is far more profound than the way it puts it. The issue divided the left in the USSR at the time and it continues to divide the left and I think it is reasonable to continue the discussion. The differences which are crucial are:

> (1) The attitude to Marxist parties in other parts of the world: Stalinism reduced them to agents of the Soviet Union, who basically did their best for the Soviet Union as a national state at the expense of the revolution in their own countries. That is putting it nicely. In contrast, the left opposition was determined to assist and base its policy on the revolution outside the USSR. Stalinism effectively killed the revolution down to the present, once it took power.

> (2) One cannot build anything approaching socialism in one country, unless one redefines socialism. There is, of course, an empirical reality, which Monty continues to avoid. Socialism in one country is the doctrine of a rising elite/pseudo-class/bureaucracy (whatever term one prefers) which justifies that new social group expropriating the revolution itself. The empirical reality was the emergence of this new social group. The structure which was being built in the twenties was a combination of a market and a bureaucratic form. Where was the socialist element?

> (3) The point is that the building of socialism is not an isolated or technical act but a social process in which the social relations must move towards socialism with the elimination of the market, abolition of the old form of the division of labour, with everyone moving in and out of administration and everyone being involved in the construction and governing of that

society. Nothing like that was occurring in the Soviet Union, nor could it. The elementary conditions were absent. Socialism requires a) a movement towards abundance, and not scarcity to the point of famine, b) a highly industrialised country with the most advanced technology and not a backward agricultural country with little industry, c) a highly educated and skilled workforce which is highly motivated by its integrated participation at all levels and not a dictatorial regime and d) an economic interchange with other countries to permit use of the international division of labour, without which any country would have a lower level of productivity than capitalism. The most that could be done, in the context of the USSR, was to try to preserve those political forms which could be conducive towards the formation of a transition to socialism, for an historically short time, provided the conditions moved in favour of socialism in Europe.

Monty's conception of the left opposition also trying to build socialism in the USSR is really a caricature of their position. Trotsky justified his refusal to take power on the grounds that he would then have had to take the same road as Stalin because he would have been the prisoner of the rising 'elite'.

Monty: Hillel reproaches me with 'caricature' in saying that Trotsky committed himself in the 1920s to work to build up socialism in the USSR. Not so! Trotsky began his *Towards Socialism or Capitalism?*: 'The State Planning Commission has published the control figures of the Soviet national economy for the financial year 1925/26. This may sound dry and bureaucratic, but in the dry columns of figures and the equally dry explanations of them, we can hear the glorious music of socialism in growth' (a metaphor, incidentally, used by Mikoyan at the 19th CPSU congress—Stalin's last—in 1952!). *The Platform of the Joint Opposition* (1927) emphasises: 'anyone who, attempting either directly or indirectly to support us, shall deny the proletarian character of our party or our state, and the socialist character of construction in the Soviet Union, will be ruthlessly opposed and rejected by us'.

How to characterise the form of society that was actually built or being built under Stalin is, of course, an extremely complex subject, deserving of another debate. In that, I shall certainly find myself sharing with Hillel the premise that the Stalinist regime was at best a monstrous bureaucratic distortion of the deeply democratic society for which socialists should strive.

Francis: I have two problems with Hillel's view. First, historically, revolutions do not spread like wildfire. They break out in an individual country as a result of that country's specific political, economic and social problems, and have ripples or echoes elsewhere, but nothing more. That is true of all the great revolutions since the 1640s. The 'domino effect' can be seen in anti-colonial struggles, but not in social revolutions. Second, by making 'spreading the revolution' the overriding concern of any post-revolutionary power, it obscures a very real practical problem: how do you ensure the post-revolutionary system will be more desirable than its predecessor? If there is a good chance it will be worse, all your appeals to spread the revolution will fall on deaf ears. Even most German workers in 1919 appeared to prefer their lot to what was going on in Soviet Russia at that time. I cannot blame them. I do not disagree at all with Hillel's description of the necessary conditions for socialism. What puzzles me is Hillel's enduring sympathy with Bolshevism, which seized power in a country with none of these conditions, at a time (1917) when the war and its attendant destruction had meant that in no country were all of these conditions present.

Hillel: Monty has correctly quoted Trotsky against me, when I argued that there was a considerable difference between the concept of socialism in one country and Trotsky's and the left opposition's ideas of holding out in the USSR. Trotsky, I think, argued that the state remained proletarian and so socialist in some sense, for a very long time even after his expulsion from the USSR, but he distinguished between the state and the ruling group and also between the state and developments in the economy. As regards the latter he talked of two tendencies: a socialist tendency and a capitalist tendency, in the same book, *Towards Capitalism or Socialism?* He had made that distinction in his famous Scissors Crisis speech in 1923 at the 12th Party Congress. He said that NEP was the arena of conflict between the proletariat exemplified in planning and the bourgeoisie operating through the market. He, therefore, made planning the basis of the advance to socialism. But we have to be careful to interpret what he was saying under conditions of increasing control by Stalin. The book itself is very obviously self-censored in that it has left out his previous and later arguments on the nature of planning and the nature of bureaucracy. Trotsky is pushing the concept of planning as the only way for the proletariat to maintain power. He makes that very clear in the second half of the 12th Congress speech in 1923. Nonetheless, even in the booklet cited he does point out, in the last section, that an isolated Russia with a revived international capitalism would find it very difficult to survive, even without any military intervention. There are two uses of the word socialist here. A movement can be socialist and a society can be socialist. Trotsky is using the word in the first sense but applying it to the struggle going on within the Soviet Union.

As regards Francis's points, I agree that any revolution must start somewhere and that might mean that it is isolated for a time until it breaks out or ceases to exist. I also agree absolutely that no one will want to accept a revolution which makes things worse for the majority. That does mean, of course, that a socialist revolution must begin to put its principles into effect as soon as possible. I do not think that we can conclude that there is a general law of revolutions which says that it will not spread from its initial point. The socialist revolution is very different from previous revolutions precisely because capitalism has integrated the world economy and destroyed all previous systems. It is also different in that it is the first in which mankind will consciously and radically reshape society, abolishing all forms of exploitation. The Russian Revolution did not spread precisely because the bourgeoisie took very strong measures to avoid it spreading and in that process helped change the nature of the revolution itself.

Reviews

Books to be remembered (5)

John Peet, *The Long Engagement. Memoirs of a Cold War legend*, with an introduction by Len Deighton, London, 1989, 242pp.

John Peet's parents joined the Society of Friends soon after their marriage in 1910. His father was a journalist, and in 1916—a year or so after John was born—he was called up for military service. Along with other pacifists he refused orders, and he also refused non-combatant work, so he went to prison. It was mostly hard labour—in the full meaning of the term—and he was not released until the spring of 1919. He then returned to journalism and also became much involved with various Quaker charities.

John Peet records a pleasant childhood within 'a pervasive but not too oppressively Quaker atmosphere of tolerance and good will towards all men, and a deep conviction that everybody would be good if they only had the chance'. John became political in his early teens and like many of his contemporaries was attracted towards the Soviet Union for what was then accepted to be the rapid growth of the Russian economy against the background of world slump in the capitalist world. Although Peet never held a communist party card he remained influenced by communist ideas throughout his life.

While still at school (Saffron Walden and then Bootham) he became involved with Esmond Romilly's journal *Out of Bounds*, and his account in this book is a useful addition to that of Jessica Mitford's *Hons and Rebels* (ch.10). When he left school he first became a cub reporter on his local newspaper and then, at the age of twenty, he began his unusual career. For what he thought were political reasons he joined the Brigade of Guards on a four-year contract and then bought himself out at the end of the first three months for the agreed sum of £20. For the next eighteen months he lived a more or less down-and-out life in central Europe

(Vienna and Prague), mostly teaching English when in luck. Then, in the summer of 1937, he went to Spain to join the English-speaking International Brigade. He was on active service, with intermissions for sickness, until late October 1938 when all the remaining Brigadiers were repatriated. He spent a year in England, doing odd jobs, was refused a commission in the RAF in the summer of 1939 (when war was obviously coming) and before the end of the year had enlisted in the Palestine Police, for reasons not wholly clear.

His account of Palestine in the war years is interesting. He was fairly soon moved into the Criminal Investigation Department (CID), out of uniform and into civilian clothes, and during his last two years he got himself seconded to the news department of Jerusalem Radio. It was a most useful training for his future journalism. Come the end of the war, Peet, who had tried several times to return to Britain, was now able to return to London and was taken on by Reuters for a trial period as sub-editor of the European desk. Peet was a good journalist, his abilities were soon recognised and because of his command of German he was sent to Vienna. It was only five months after the end of the war in Europe and in his words 'foreign correspondents from the media of the four occupying powers lived a life of cushioned ease amid the ruins and hunger of the Austrian capital'.

Peet learned a great deal during his period in Vienna and became on good terms with many of the Provisional government. In particular his most useful contact was Ernst Fischer, a member of the Communist Party in the 1930s, in Moscow during the war years as a radio propagandist and now Minister of Education. In December 1946 Peet was moved to Warsaw. Reuters were well satisfied with him but he only stayed a few months, because of currency difficulties, and then, because of his now well-recognised abilities, he found himself in Berlin. The city was, of course, one of the most important news centres in the world. From December 1946 Peet worked in one of the largest of Reuters' foreign offices, with three or four full-time British correspondents, three German journalists and a well-organised office.

In a couple of years he was promoted to head the unit but by the late 1940s he was beginning to be increasingly concerned with the rumours that the western powers were seriously considering re-arming West Germany. Peet was increasingly conscious of the failure of western Germany to denazify itself, as against the Democratic Republic which had eradicated Nazis from the police, the judiciary and education. So, being the odd but extremely interesting personality that he was, he decided to go east. On 12 June 1950 the Government Information Office of the newly established German Democratic Republic convened a news conference on an undisclosed subject. Peet then proceeded to read his prepared statement to the effect that he was resigning from Reuters and moving over to the east. His conclusion, after providing the detailed political reasons for his decision, was summed up in the words:

> I simply cannot consent to take part any longer in the warmongering which threatens not only the Soviet Union and the People's Democracies but which also is well on the way to converting my motherland, Britain, into a powerless American colony.

It was a sensational statement that went round the world. Peet had made sensible arrangements before his departure from Reuters, and the London office issued a public statement insisting that his journalistic reports could always be considered accurate, and this was the general opinion outside the gutter press. As Len Deighton wrote in his introduction:

> Peet was a newspaper man of the old school, a type now virtually extinct. Such men were doubters, their hard-nosed disbelief based upon years of news gathering and wide-ranging knowledge. For them the story was a means to an end. What they despatched to editors and wire services were only the hard facts. The rumours and guesses—often defamatory and far more illuminating—were exchanged over drinks at the nearest bar, and that was what made such men rewarding to be with.

Peet lived in the German Democratic Republic for 39 years before he wrote his memoirs. He became well known through the *Democratic German Report* which was produced fortnightly and delivered free to all who wanted it. Its latest circulation was 30,000 and it went round the world. The *German Report*—it was Peet's idea—began in 1952 and ceased publication in 1975. Peet always did most of the writing, and it offered a lively political analysis concentrating especially in its early years on the infiltration of former leading Nazis into the administrative structures of Federal Germany.

Peet was never a cardholding member of the Communist Party and, like so many, he hoped passionately that 1968 would see a new beginning. In his final chapter he offers his readers an insight into his moral position. He notes that in the 1930s when party members were 'upset or mystified by inexplicable events in the Soviet Union, they were often assuaged with the glib phrase that you could not make an omelette without breaking eggs…But in later years the broken eggs became all too numerous, and the omelette failed to make a satisfactory existence. So where is the omelette today?'

He answered his own question in measured terms and he concluded his book with the line:

But where is the omelette. I am still looking.

This is a book full of interesting pieces of history, written by a careful journalist. It is worth reading.

John Saville
Professor emeritus at the University of Hull and president of the Oral History Society

The end of the Enlightenment

Richard Sakwa *Postcommunism* (Open University Press, 1999, Buckingham), vi+153pp., ISBN 0-33520-057-5, £10.99 pbk.

In *Postcommunism* Richard Sakwa sets himself the unenviable task of ordering, and establishing as a coherent field of study, the morass of historical material, discredited theory and unanswered questions bequeathed by the Marxist-Leninist tradition since its final demise with the collapse of Soviet Union.

From the outset Sakwa is at pains to emphasise both the universal significance and the varied manifestations of the 'Postcommunist' era that has arisen since the 'velvet revolutions' of 1989–91: the respective ends of 'Communism' (understood as the *philosophical* legacy left by Karl Marx and his successors to aspirant revolutionaries the world over) and 'communism' (labelled in the more modest lower case to denote twentieth-century experiments in 'actually existing socialism') represent the exhaustion, in both theory and practice, of the trajectory of Enlightenment revolutionism concerned with the betterment of humanity by means of egalitarianism and rational socio-economic planning.

Sakwa attempts in the course of seven short chapters to sketch the characteristics of Postcommunism as a distinct academic field: hence, along with the decline in interest in Communist thought, Postcommunism denotes the end of any communist party's monopoly over politics, economics and society; the gradual and tentative emergence of political pluralism; the uneven introduction of elements of the market into a heavily bureaucratised economy (and the corruption resulting from this process); the liberalisation of prices in accordance with the transition toward a market economy; rapid changes in class structure, increasing disparities in income and a shift in emphasis from industrial and manufacturing activity to the service sector; the coexistence and hybridity of new (western liberal-democratic) and old cultural, political, institutional and social forms; an initial openness to the global economic system; and tensions between ethnic/nationalist and more cosmopolitan impulses in identity formation and political organisation.

Yet the very attempt at such a formidable undertaking, particularly within the constraints of a one hundred and fifty page undergraduate text, results at times in sweeping generalisations that detract from the otherwise admirable marshalling of information in this concise and accessible work. Ultimately, it is the very notion of *constructing* a unified field from a plethora of otherwise diverse sources that is the problem of this text: in delineating such a field within a single explanatory schema, significant omissions are unavoidable if the facts are to neatly fit the theory. Such theoretical oversimplification is evident in the second chapter, 'The Long Transcendence', when, having suggested that Communism was haunted with the prospect of its own 'transcendence' by the dual 'Spectres' of revolutionary and reformist revisionism (typified by the anarchism and left-Marxism of figures such as Bakunin and Luxemburg, and by social-democrats such as Bernstein respectively), Sakwa continues by contradicting this thesis with the assertion that Communism and communism were only recently 'transcended' with the failure in 1968 of the Prague Spring to realise 'socialism with a human face', and with the literal collapse of the Soviet bloc twenty-one years later. Hence, in the absence of a clear definition, confusion arises over the central notion of 'transcendence' which, in referring both to Marxism-Leninism's various socialist competitors and to its theoretical and practical eclipse by capitalism and liberal-democracy, is endowed with two quite different meanings.

In the chapter entitled 'Post-Communism in practice', Sakwa explores the failure of communism to deliver the economic, political, cultural and social fruits of modernity to the extent that they had been realised in the post-war West, hence forfeiting any sources of legitimacy that might have been claimed in purely functional terms as those of the most efficient socio-economic system. Yet Sakwa fails to identify the *philosophical* resistance that arose toward the non-Marxian approaches that would have been necessary in order to administer successfully such increasingly complex socialist societies, an unwillingness to re-think communism in the complex and decentred form necessary to the evolution of a non-capitalist modernity: the post-war era saw the burgeoning of interest on both sides of the Iron Curtain in system-theoretic and cybernetic orientated research concerned with the problems of the political and economic 'steering' of advanced industrial (and increasingly post-industrial) societies. Such research on the application of cybernetic thinking to the problems of socialist planning was repressed by the party–state apparatus of the Soviet bloc for its, correctly perceived, threat to the Marxist orthodoxies on which the regimes based their legitimacy. Thus, in omitting the short lived 'cybernetic revolution' that occurred within the Soviet academic system, Sakwa neglects a significant post-war 'Spectre' to the communist project that fleetingly promised an alternative Postcommunism to the liberal-democracy of the present day.

Sakwa continues his ruminations in the chapter entitled 'The Post-Communist experience' by arguing that the non-Eurasian communisms of Vietnam, Cuba and China owe their survival in the Postcommunist world to the legitimacy that remains from the memory of popular revolution in conjunction with a war of national liberation. Sakwa also explores the varied fortunes of the world's remaining communist parties, reflecting on examples such as the relative success of the Japanese CP (which polled 13 per cent of the vote in the elections of 1996), and the experiments in parliamentary-pluralism with a humanist worldview of the Eurocommunist parties. Yet Sakwa notes correctly how, despite considerable nostalgia in certain quarters for the certainties of the communist past (reflected in the success of Germany's Party of Democratic Socialism), the overall story, from the Naxalites of East India to the beleaguered French CP, is one of defensive political stances in the face of the social dislocation caused by the global market, positions devoid of the intellectual depth and revolutionary certainty that characterised communist organisations in their heyday. Yet this otherwise comprehensive survey of Communist politics in a Postcommunist era is unfortunately marred by a single noteworthy error: Sakwa asserts that Gennadii Zyuganov's Communist Party of the Russian Federation (CPRF) lacks a significant mass base, yet it is actually the case that the CPRF is virtually the only contemporary Russian party with a cohesive and committed membership and activist base.

Sakwa is particularly insightful in his comparison of the transitions from communism to democracy with the transitions from authoritarianism of recent decades in Spain, Portugal and Greece. The chapter 'Post-Communism in practice' outlines how differing starting points on the road to capitalism and democracy have resulted in divergent outcomes such as the relative success of the central European Visegrad States in contrast to Russia and Eurasia, the alternative choices by individual states of 'shock therapy' or gradualism in the installation of capitalist systems, the tendencies toward presidential rather than parliamentary systems among the further eastern and southern transition states, and the difficulties experienced by the

Central Asian Republics whose tendencies toward dictatorship Sakwa compares to those that have afflicted Africa's post-colonial transitions.

The closing chapters of *Postcommunism* are the most accomplished of the text in relinquishing the attempt to encapsulate the field in all its complexity, and offering instead a philosophical overview that succeeds especially well in evoking the zeitgeist of the era.

In a particularly sensitive and well argued section of the text, Sakwa turns his attention to the central moral question of the Postcommunist era: whether any genuinely humanitarian aspects can be salvaged from the revolutionary communist tradition at all. Of particular interest in this respect is the 'Historians' Debate' of the 1980s between Jürgen Habermas and commentators such as Ernst Nolte who argued that the Nazi Holocaust, if examined in relation to the 'Asiatic deed' of Stalinism, no longer deserved its exceptional status amongst crimes against humanity, a shift in perspective relativising Nazism and problematising revolutionary communism at the same time. After a detailed examination of the debate, Sakwa concludes in line with Habermas that the crimes of Nazism were ultimately of a *qualitatively* different order to those of any other regime.

Toward the close of the book, Sakwa reflects on the vacuum in critical and holistic political thinking left in the absence of Marxism, and goes on to illustrate the ubiquity of forms of neoliberal instrumentalism and relativist postmodernism in contemporary discussion. Yet Sakwa's comparison of Postcommunism with a host of other 'posts' (including post-colonialism and, particularly, postmodernism) fails to emphasise the critical political positions once regarded as inseparable from these theories, particularly among the heterogeneous groupings on the left in the 1970s and 1980s: hence, rather than being a contemporary of postmodernism, Postcommunism, both as theory and zeitgeist, can be regarded as postmodernism's successor in representing the concrete realisation of consumerism, neoliberal economics and the abandonment of Enlightenment Universalism that could only grow to ubiquity with the fall of the Berlin Wall. Indeed, Sakwa argues that in representing the triumph of neoliberalism in the absence of democratic socialism (an ideal finally abandoned with the failure of the 1968 protests in Prague) and of activism by independent groupings in civil society (a flowering of citizen activism that paradoxically thrived in the last years of communism, such as in the Czech Civic Forum or Poland's Solidarity, only to dwindle under capitalism) the Postcommunist era offers only a superficial realisation of Enlightenment ideals.

Shivdeep Singh Grewal
Open University

Age of Reform

M.J. Turner, *British Politics in the Age of Reform* (Manchester University Press, Manchester, 1999), x + 230pp., ISBN 0-71905-186-X, £13.99 pbk.

To the casual modern observer, Charles James Fox's statue strikes an incongruous note, secluded under the trees in London's Bloomsbury Square. Raised in 1816, a decade after his death and a year after the close of the French Wars, which he had once so eloquently opposed, it was judged safe— at last—to grant him a memorial and to portray him as a Senator of the Roman Republic, though one it should be noted who firmly recognised the *Pax Britannia* over, and above, the *Pax Romana*. Consequently, his bronzed hand was sculpted resting comfortably upon the scroll that mythically embodied all of England's liberties—Magna Carta—while his bulky frame was sculptured, anachronistically, in flowing classical robes. Rather unfortunately, to modern eyes, his face has more of the aspect of Charles Lawton in the film *Spartacus*, than of the farsighted Enlightenment statesman that his Whig supporters had originally sought to apotheosise.

Fox's reputation—traduced in recent years by Alan Bennet's *The Madness of King George*, and largely sidelined in both radical and liberal traditions since the days of Trevelyan's glorious hagiography—is once again contrasted, unfavourably, in Michael Turner's new study, with that of his great rival, the younger Pitt.[1] While Fox was tarred by 'cynical opportunism', and by a particular 'rashness and petulance' in all of his dealings, Pitt—we are told—is characterised as being 'cautious and pragmatic', 'ambitious, talented and proud...the coming man' (pp.24, 29, 42). Furthermore, Fox's love of 'friendship and pleasure' is seen as being firmly at odds with Pitt's 'serious and aloof' nature (p.33). While this approach is entirely supportable, it does, however, focus attention upon political personalities rather than upon ideologies and principles, which were thrown into an even starker relief with the advent of the French Revolution. Moreover, though the author successfully recreates something of the tension and excitement of their Commons debates, and captures the essence of the vibrant political cultures—both high and low, parliamentary and extra-parliamentary—in the period from 1783–1806, the figures of Fox and Pitt are allowed to dominate subsequent developments. Thus, although a thorough consideration is given to Pitt's role as a war leader, the able legacy of Spencer Perceval in prosecuting the struggle and in successfully provisioning the Peninsular armies is entirely overlooked.

Perhaps more surprising is Turner's revisionist account of George III's political influence. The 'old Rockingham legend about excessive royal influence' is persistently alluded to, though never comprehensively explored—or demolished—while the conduct of the King is vindicated on the dubious grounds of his political foresight in backing Pitt, at almost every turn (pp.32–3, 52). That George III had effectively destabilised English parliamentary politics for a generation, by his making and breaking of ministries, cannot be seriously doubted. His self-conception, that he was an Englishman—rather than a German prince, as his thoroughly Hanoverian predecessors had conceived themselves to be—and his desire to be far more than a titular head of state, caused enormous problems for a political elite which had grown accustomed to enjoying a relatively free rein in the construction of alliances and the formulation of policy. It was not for nothing that Fox had sighed at his encroachments upon those grey areas of Parliamentary privilege, left unresolved in the wake of the Glorious Revolution and the rise of Walpole—or that some more radical Whigs muttered darkly about the threat of a return to absolutism, and turned their eyes expectantly to the development of a new form of participatory democracy in Revolutionary France. In actual fact, it mattered little whether opposition MPs exaggerated the number of royal placemen in the Commons, or if the power of the monarchy was allowed to swiftly evaporate by the inattention, and inactivity of George IV. What did concentrate the minds of the Foxites was the potential for a dramatically refashioned, and newly self-confident, monarchy to act as the final arbiter of politics and to retard reform, or Catholic emancipation upon the merest of whims.

It is notable that Turner saves his most biting invective for the Prince Regent—'a grossly over-weight, temperamental, lazy, self-indulgent man', whose youthful 'bad habits…burst forth in all their stark ugliness' during his later life—but it is greatly to his credit that such value judgments co-exist neatly with a clear and concise exegesis of politics during the growing agitation for electoral reform (p.49). The book similarly benefits from a thorough and extremely thoughtful, survey of recent academic literature. In particular, the works of E.P. Thompson, Lewis Namier and Jonathan Clark are analysed in some depth, as being representative of the main historiographical currents and centres of debate. An analysis and brief critique is provided for each of their major works, which place them firmly within their respective ideological contexts, while a survey of recent historical literature is both valuable and comprehensive. Unfortunately, the selection of primary sources—ranging from extracts taken from Paine's *Rights of Man* to the text of one of Wellington's more visceral speeches against the extension of the franchise—though intelligently chosen, is short and somewhat cramped, shoe-horned into a brief appendix. Insufficiently well integrated into the core text of the book to provide for a really useful examination of their content, these extracts exude the rather uncomfortable impression that they were added on, almost as an afterthought, in order to conform to a publisher's stringent guidelines.

However, this should not blind us to the virtues of the study. In terms of its own explicitly stated remit: not to represent 'an exemplar of any particular school or method' but to 'indicate some of the 'new frontiers'—and the controversies surrounding them—which have influenced twentieth-century historical scholarship', the work succeeds remarkably well (p.9). It is learned, pertinent, and falls neatly in-between the short guide—as typified by the Palgrave and Routledge pamphlets—and the full scale scholarly monograph, such as those of Derry and Ehrman, which may appear overly off-putting to the cash and time strapped reader.[2] Though lacking the brilliance and penetrating forensic skills of Evans' *Forging of the Modern State*, Clark's grasp of the cultural richness of English society at the close of the eighteenth century, or the strident polemicism of Christie's *Myth and Reality*: this is still a welcome addition to the secondary literature, which provides a clear sighted overview of a highly complex and emotive period, without necessarily overturning any of the established wisdoms or advocating a radical change in the scholarly apparatus.[3] It will fall to another hand to securely reassess the nature of Fox's triumphs and excesses, and to wipe away the last stains of verdigris from his maligned and neglected monument.

1. G. O. Trevelyan, *The Early History of Charles James Fox* (London, 1881).
2. J. W. Derry, *Charles James Fox* (London, 1972); J. Ehrman, *The Younger Pitt*, 3 vols. (London, 1969, 1983 & 1996).
3. E. J. Evans, *The Forging of the Modern State, 1783–1870*, (2nd Edition, London, 1996); J.C.D. Clark, *English Society, 1688–1832* (Cambridge, 1985); and I.R. Christie, *Myth and Reality in Late Eighteenth-Century Politics* (London, 1970).

John Callow
Department of Historical and Cultural Studies, Goldsmiths College

Politics of the extreme

Nigel Copsey, *Anti-Fascism in Britain* (Macmillan Press, Basingstoke, 2000), ix+229pp., ISBN 0-33369-636-0, £28.00 hbk.
Dave Renton, *Fascism, Anti-Fascism and Britain in the 1940s* (Macmillan Press, Basingstoke, 2000), ix+203pp., ISBN 0-33376-085-9, £25.00 hbk.

These two books were published more or less simultaneously by the same publisher but given Macmillan's minimalist marketing approach towards the vast majority of its academic books, it would be unwise to read too much into this, except in so far as it reveals some growth of academic interest in British anti-fascism. Renton's book is in essence a detailed study of fascism and anti-fascism in Britain, primarily in London, between 1945 and 1951, whilst Copsey offers a general history of British anti-fascism from 1923 to 1998. Both books, whatever their flaws, are well worth reading by all with an interest in the history of British anti-fascism, since neither topic has ever been the object of a book length academic study before. It seems not only legitimate but virtually obligatory to review these two books in tandem because Copsey, after including Renton amongst a relatively small number of individuals listed in his 'Acknowledgements' (p.vii), then singles him out for attack in his 'Introduction', by emphasising 'The approach in the following study departs from Renton'(p.4). Whilst both Copsey and Renton have written on fascism on previous occasions—Renton principally on theories of fascism and Copsey on the BNP and the French FN—in both the books under review the emphasis is primarily on anti-fascism rather than on fascism itself. Renton's account of British fascism between 1945 and 1951, whilst adequate, is far from inspired and consciously opts to ignore certain types of source material, in sharp contrast to his gripping third and fourth chapters, on anti-fascism (pp.71–100) and the role of the police in the conflicts between fascists and anti-fascists (pp.101–29), which make brilliant use of primary source material, both archival and oral. In his introductory remarks setting out the rationale for his study, Renton implicitly argues the case for a more general book with Copsey's chronological range, remarking, 'As yet, there is no historical literature on anti-fascism for any period; the studies we have are partial, often limited to particular campaigns or a set area.' (p.4). Although Copsey 'seeks to provide an accessible and critical analysis of British anti-fascism' (p.1), carrying out at least in broad terms Renton's research agenda, his book is not quite what Renton would have had in mind.

There are marked political differences between the two writers. Renton writes as a proud member of the SWP, even if in this particular book, closely based on his Sheffield Ph.D. thesis, this is not quite as explicit as in some of his more popular or polemical works. Copsey's politics leave me a little baffled; his extremely confused account of both orthodox Communist and Trotskyist theories of fascism suggest he has never been a member of (or sympathiser with) any organisation on the British Marxist left. Despite his intermittent sympathy for the politics of direct action and his vociferous localism, he vehemently denies any anarchist leanings, remarking in a footnote; ' The author would like to reassure readers as a former student of the Polytechnic of North London, he is not a "graduate in the art of anarchy"'(p.214). Yet he has far too many axes to grind to be classified as a more or less apolitical academic in pursuit of a new and under-researched topic; there is a clear animus against the CPGB, at least in every one of its pre-1941 incarnations, and against the SWP in all its incarnations down to the present day—he hammers the SWP for street-fighting tendencies in Lewisham in June 1977 (an incident about which he makes tendentious remarks on the basis of inadequate research), but he is equally derogatory about the relative moderation of the Anti-Nazi League in 1978–79, which he calls 'a marriage of convenience between the SWP and the Labour Party' (p.152). To label Copsey as a consistent liberal is as misleading as calling him apolitical, for no mainstream liberal would quote a notoriously fiery radical like Sivanandan with approval (p.183), at least not without some disclaimer emphasising the specific context. It is possible that Copsey's interest in anti-fascism arose out of the Patrick Harrington affair at PNL (1983–85), but his interesting account of this episode (pp.154–7) rather oddly does not make it clear whether he was a student at PNL during the relevant years, although his age at the time of the incident makes it a plausible hypothesis.

Provoked as I have been by Copsey's negative views of both the ANL in the late 1970s and the significance of the Battle of Cable Street in 1936 into dwelling on his own political leanings, I feel compelled to point out that his book has its virtues. It draws our attention to the fact that the CPGB's militant anti-fascism goes right back to October 1923, when it disrupted the inaugural meeting of the British Fascists. Whilst Copsey's attempt to trivialise such actions during the 1920s indicates his almost total ignorance of the European context, evident from his failure to understand that the British Fascists' kidnapping of Harry Pollitt in March 1925, far from being a mere sensationalist stunt, was inspired by the Italian fascists' kidnapping (and murder) of the Socialist leader Matteotti in June 1924, his mention of these actions serves to demonstrate the longevity of the CPGB's anti-fascist tradition, so often wrongly ascribed to the Seventh Congress of Comintern and the turn to the Popular Front. Similarly, it is very interesting to learn of the existence of the 62 Group of Jewish anti-fascists (founded in 1962), which revived the traditions of the 43 Group (1946–1950), about which Renton tells us rather more than Copsey does. Although Copsey, unlike Renton, intends to exculpate the record of the Board of Deputies, an attentive reader of his work will be inclined to see the tension between the Jewish establishment and Jews interested in pursuing serious anti-fascist work as a constant feature of British life from the 1930s to the present. Copsey's accounts of the clashes at Southall in April 1979 (p.149) and Welling in October 1993 (pp.174–6) expose the Metropolitan Police's enthusiastic use of massive violence against anti-fascists, and their institutional propensity to lie, cover-up, obstruct inquiries and shamelessly manipulate the media against the anti-fascists. Given Copsey's acceptance that the police version of Blair Peach's violent death is totally untenable and that the police, not the demonstrators, initiated the violence at Welling, it is, to say the least, surprising that he is willing to accept police versions of events in the 1930s and 1940s in a fairly uncritical way, taking issue with historians like Renton who have punctured the myth of police neutrality, and endorsing assertions by historians such as Mosley's hagiographer Lord Skidelsky and Cullen, whose credibility as a serious scholar of fascism has been placed in doubt by his contribution to the journal *Comrade* (published by the Friends of Oswald Mosley).

Renton's book, whilst concentrating on a much narrower time frame, has more to recommend it. It offers a balanced appraisal of the roles of the 43 Group and the CPGB in the anti-fascist movement of 1945–51, acknowledging that both made a major contribution, albeit at different times and in different ways. Whilst anxious to rescue the anti-fascist activities of the Trotskyist Revolutionary Communist Party from historical oblivion, he is sufficiently objective to acknowledge that their role was a very minor one by comparison with that of the CPGB, the 43 Group and a number of other organisations. The only major issue on which his instincts as a political activist get the better of his judgement as a historian is over the question of using oral evidence from surviving fascists or ex-fascists. Obviously, as a Marxist of partly Jewish descent, he may not necessarily have found many willing interviewees (although Raphael Samuel's experience with Arthur Harding suggests that he may have had some luck), but in principle their testimony, used critically and tested against other sources, is as useful as any other. (The fact that, as Renton argues, some other historians may have used it uncritically, is not an over-riding objection).

Tobias Abse
Lecturer in Modern European History at Goldsmiths College

Secret life

Janet Todd, *The Secret Life of Aphra Behn* (London, Pandora Press, 2000), 545pp., ISBN 0-86358-416-0, £11.99 pbk.

Janet Todd's biography of the Restoration playwright, poet and Jill of all literary trades, Aphra Behn, is a fast-moving and, for the most part, absorbing study of a significant and extremely colourful figure on the English literary scene in the reigns of Charles and James II. It is inevitably a somewhat speculative account since, as Todd admits in the opening paragraph of her Introduction: 'What is securely known about her outside her writings could be summed up in a page'. Todd's approach is to draw on documents she has rediscovered in archives from Behn's period as an English government spy in Holland, her own copious writings, and references to her by fellow writers, to piece together a picture of Behn and her circle in the wider context of the literary, political, intellectual and social life of the era.

Aphra Behn's significance is not so much in the literary value of her works, as in the fact that she was a woman who made a living from writing. Her significance in this respect has been exaggerated. As Elaine Hobby has established, Hannah Wolley (or Woolley) was 'a woman with an independent income from her writing predating Aphra Behn, so often cited as the first professional woman writer, by a decade.' Behn was, however, the first recognised female literary figure, and Todd is right to call her 'England's first all-round woman writer'.

She wrote, or adapted, in all 19 plays, a considerable amount of poetry and court pindarics, numerous stories, scientific translations and translations of French and Latin poetry. Todd even argues that a case could be made for regarding her prose fiction 'masterpiece' 'Love-Letters Between a Nobleman and His Sister' as 'the first novel'. Much of her work, though, was produced at great speed and with little pretension to originality. She was never able to earn or cajole enough money to maintain her lifestyle comfortably for long at a stretch, and her attitude to play writing is neatly summed up by Todd: 'She herself was writing to make money by pleasing those who paid for their seats. Spectators came to the theatre from idleness and desire for amusement, not for edification.' She was justifiably accused of plagiarism, and her most celebrated play, 'The Rover', was largely lifted from an Interregnum play by a member of her literary circle. She was essentially, as Todd describes her, 'a quick and efficient adapter of plays'. Perhaps her greatest theatrical innovation was to write a play, near the end of her life, which was 'sheer farce, the nearest England had seen to pantomime'.

Todd discusses each of her plays, carefully teasing out what each of them might reveal about her life, her interests and her political and philosophical beliefs. In the process a fascinating insight into a remarkable era in English history and a strongly individual and daring woman emerges. The early chapters of the book, however, deal with the period before she became a professional writer. The focus of these chapters is inevitably on the years she spent as a spy, after the Restoration of the Stuart monarchy. All the events in her life before 1660 Behn kept shrouded. The only person who claimed to have known Behn as a child was Colonel Thomas Colepeper, to whom her mother had been wet-nurse. There is evidence that her father may have been a barber. The section of the book dealing with her supposed spying commission in Surinam, possibly arranged by Colepeper, lacks the vividness of detail which characterises much of the book. It is not even certain whether she went to Surinam at all: the main evidence is in the knowledge she shows of life and conditions in the territory, in her story 'Oroonoko'. Even of her marriage, to a John Behn, who may have been a slaver, and which may have taken place on the journey back from Surinam, nothing concrete is known. Todd speculates that she probably married him for money, and quickly tired of him, and pertinently comments that his early disappearance from her life 'was happy for literature, since a seventeenth-century husband is unlikely to have accepted a commercially play-writing wife.'

Behn's period as a government spy in Holland, after the Second Dutch War broke out in 1664, is well-documented in state archives, and Todd offers the reader a fascinating account of the frustrations of espionage in the period. Her job was to meet a former friend of hers, now in Holland, and secure him as an English informant. As she said herself , it was a mission 'Unusual with my sex, or to my years.' It seems she was chosen with the objective of using her feminine charms on her potential informant. In the event the whole business turned into a nightmare, and she ended up writing increasingly impassioned letters to England pleading for money to pay her ever-increasing debts. This became a depressingly regular feature of her life in the years that followed: as a writer of plays, and then of poetic panegyrics to royalty, and finally in pouring out translations purely for money. As Todd points out, such problems did not concern her principal contemporary literary rival, Katherine Philips, well-connected and with influential patrons.

The impressions created in the book of Behn's personal beliefs are a curious mixture of extreme political conservatism, and unconventionality in her personal life and her sexual and social attitudes, even in the context of the libertine and libidinous Restoration era, the detailed portrayal of which is one of the fascinations of the book. While she scorned 'the merchant values of thrift, sobriety, moderation and wifeliness', and in her poem 'the Golden Age' she evoked, as the opposite of utopia, 'the leaden world of money, war, trade, merchandise and sexuality as commodity', she was a life-long royalist and Tory. She never showed much concern for the sufferings of the poor, and expressed an increasing fear, in her writings, of democracy, mob rule and anarchy. In her story 'Oroonoko' the black hero is a martyr to unworthy popular rule, and the restoration of aristocratic control overcomes the evils of democracy. In her propagandist play 'The Roundheads' royalism becomes synonymous with virtue. No doubt she had a genuine belief in the importance of preserving hierarchy, but it is difficult to resist the feeling that there may have been an element of opportunism in her political philosophy. As Todd neatly puts it, when Behn remained a supporter of the impossibly autocratic James II to the end of his reign: 'It may have been the consonance of their confused opinions that made Behn one of [James'] most devoted followers: conversely it may have been her desire to be considered James' devoted follower that made her express such opinions.'

In other respects Aphra Behn was very much a free-thinker. In her attitude to religion she was close to what the seventeenth century termed 'atheism'. She so disliked clerical power that she was closer to republicans than royalists in her mocking of priests and their law. As a playwright and, more remarkably, in her poetry, she was notorious for her explicitness about sex. In particular, she returned frequently to the phenomenon of the male rake. She was fascinated by such scandalous libertines as the Earl of Rochester, described by Todd as having 'mythologised himself as promiscuous, drunken, misogynous and frivolous', and in her later writings she explored the concept of the female rake. Her ultimate conclusion to this question was that such a being was impossible; as Todd puts it: 'Transgressing the social bonds and the norms, she became a parasite, beyond the pale, while the male rake remained deep within it'.

Behn's own sexual and emotional life was dominated by one decidedly perverse relationship, with a bisexual libertine named Jack Hoyle, whose 'enjoyment was in the humbling of female pride' and who kept her at a distance for years. Interestingly, Todd argues that such enforced physical and emotional independence aided Behn immeasurably as a writer: 'As her works tumbled out over the next years, it almost seems as though Hoyle were both lamented and used. Without such obsessive love, Behn probably would not have written much of what she did write and without the freedom he forced on her she may not have continued writing at all.'

The final picture which emerges of Aphra Behn and her life and times is of a vivacious and original woman of steely determination and great strength of will, forging a life for herself in a man's world. As Janet Todd puts it at the end of this thoroughly engaging biography: 'Before the demonisation of this brutal and glittering age, Aphra Behn experienced to the full its libertarian and libertine possibilities; in it she had been allowed to experiment with styles of living and writing in the way few women could do or would wish to do for centuries to come.'

Peter Turner
Lecturer in English at Brockenhurst College

Non-identical twins

David Childs, *The Two Red Flags: European social democracy and Soviet communism since 1945* (Routledge, London, 2000), xiii+187pp., ISBN 0-415-17181-4, £11.99 pbk.

Acknowledged as an authoritative political historian of the west European left and east European communist state system, David Childs's latest work offers a succinct chronological account of the intertwined and conflictual histories of communism and social democracy in Europe since the end of the Second World War.

The imagery in Childs's title will undoubtedly cause some readers to pause at the outset. Many may question whether the author wants us to conceive of social democracy, in its more left-wing manifestations, as part of a political continuum which extends to include eastern European state communism: in effect, that the two flags, made up from different patterns, are cut from the same 'red cloth'? Others might suggest that communist parties operating within postwar west European democracies could have been granted a pennant or two of their own. Activists and historians allied to the 'new left' and from within the trotskyite tradition, will protest that, alongside the red flags identified by Childs, other emblems have been raised by socialists in the long decades of the Cold War—insignia which have jostled persistently (if without much success) to eject the banners of 'left social democracy' and 'official communism' from their position at the head of the 'workers' march towards socialism'.

Yet there can be little question that the terrain on which the whole of the postwar European left struggled, until the fall of the Wall, was defined by the towering presence of the twin monoliths of labourism and official communism, and it is with the political consequences of this powerful polarity that Childs is principally concerned. As a result, enthusiasts for historical counter-factuals will find little to occupy them here. The author also cuts short his speculation on how the left in the post-Soviet, 'new Labour' Europe might develop in the future.

In his opening chapter, Childs surveys briefly the development of the european Marxist and socialist left in the years immediately prior to 1939, revisiting the collapse of the Second International and establishing the significance of October 1917. No sharp delineation of the rupture within the left tradition emerges; neither does a clear definition of the essential nature of either social democracy or Soviet communism. What is clarified is Childs' view that the 'insurrectionism' of the Bolsheviks and others was aberrant, and that the rise to predominance of 'evolutionary' socialism in western Europe had a strong pragmatic and ethical base, which helped to point the movement away from the horrors of the gulags and the cheka. Childs then turns quickly to the very different types of 'socialism' that rose in eastern and western Europe as the continent emerged transformed from the dark war years.

In the history that follows, Childs does make passing reference to other, lesser, left currents, yet his primary focus remains the parties and movements engaged in the struggle for governmental power on both sides of the 'iron curtain'.

In attempting to condense the complexities of five decades and more of european left history into a narrative of fewer than 200 pages, Childs sets himself an ambitious task. In crisp and robust prose, Childs's chronology divides that history into ten chapters arranged around such themes as the place of social democracy in postwar west European recovery; the imposition of stalinist orthodoxy in eastern Europe during the late 1940s and 1950s; the 'climax' of European social democracy in the 1970s and early 1980s; and the rise of Gorbachov, the fall of the Soviet Union and the 'resurgence' of a reconfigured social democracy in the 1990s.

The tight constraints of space here demand economy and precision in the telling of the tale. In general Childs succeeds in this, distilling the headline news and isolating the pivotal moments of this history, at both the general level and within individual countries and state systems. Indeed, when Childs turns to describe the evolution of *glasnost* and *perestroika* in the eastern bloc, the urgency of the text serves to emphasise the relentless pace of political, economic and social reform, the unpredictability of the process and the very brittleness and vulnerability of the regimes overwhelmed by the momentum of change. Inevitably, though, the necessity for brevity can only mean that, at other times, developments and events are compressed or set aside, simplicities are imposed, awkwardnesses are ironed out, and conjectures remain unexplored. The twin convulsions of 1956, and their impact on left politics in both eastern and western Europe; the Sino-Soviet split; the emergence of eurocommunism; Mitterand's turn from Keynesianism to austerity in France; the transformation of 'old' labour and communist parties across the continent - these and any number of other momentous occurrences can only be afforded a few pages each.

The question, therefore, is whether the reach and the range of the book compensates for the preclusion of extended analytical discussion and the absence of enriching detail and colour? As both an introductory and a reference work, this offers a highly readable outline history of the twin mass movements of the European left in the last half of the twentieth century, that address the role of its parties, leaders, figureheads and ideologues in shaping and creating that history. In this endeavour, it delivers, even though few readers are likely to agree with each and every interpretative judgement that the author reaches along the way. What still remains noticeable is how rarely 'the masses' appear in these pages, other than as the aggregated totals in tables of electoral results, or as the force that appears suddenly to sweep in the new order or sweep out the old. If that is explicable, given the book's priorities and the limitations of space, the neglect of 'the workers' in a history of what claimed to be 'workers' parties' still feels like the most significant omission of all.

Richard Cross
University of Manchester

One of us?

John Newsinger, *Orwell's Politics* (Palgrave, Basingstoke, 2001), xi+178pp., ISBN 0-33396-858-1, £14.99 pbk.

John Newsinger's *Orwell's Politics* was well received at its original publication in 1999. Its reprinting in paperback allows a reconsideration of its strengths and weaknesses, which remain unchanged. The minor weaknesses are stylistic. There is occasional repetition and looseness of organisation in the text, and a degree of lumpiness as if Newsinger had material which, relevant or not, and this applies particularly to his US material on *The Partisan Review* and *Politics*, he is determined to get in come what may. Newsinger can get as cross as any old buffer when he seriously dislikes an argument, and as paternalistic as they come when judging the work of others. He deeply dislikes the volume edited by Christopher Norris, *Outside the Myth*, and on one of his several forays against it, dismisses it as 'an unholy alliance of feminists, cultural theorists, and old-fashioned Stalinists'. It sounds quite like Orwell on fruit juice drinkers, pacifists, and sandal-wearers. The paternal style emerges in judgments such as that on Daphne Patai: 'thoroughly wrongheaded' and someone whose arguments are 'pushed too far'. This is not just a matter of dialectical grumpiness. The differences between Newsinger, and Patai and other feminists, are important and deserve dealing with by discussion rather than by diktat. This weakness in style is part of a more substantial weakness. Newsinger's response to criticisms from feminists, despite a promise at the start of the book to discuss them more substantially, is insufficiently argued. And given that his judgment of Orwell's account of the failure of socialists to appeal to the British people is also dismissed as 'thoroughly wrongheaded.' Newsinger has too little to say about Orwell's conception of the role of the working class, or of the extent to which that conception was marred by nationalist particularism. This is increasingly relevant in the current discussion of nationalism as a basis for political action and social justice.

The strengths of the book are that it draws on a wider range of Orwell's writings, specifically his writings in the USA, than other commentators have done, and in so doing clearly establishes the radical, Trotskyite, and anarchist aspect of his thinking. This is a valuable exercise of pulling the interpretative joystick to the left. Orwell was critical of the whole Bolshevik tradition, and did not exempt Trotsky. So it was a Trotskyism without Trotsky, Trotskyish rather than Trotskyite. Another of the book's strengths is Newsinger's robust defence of Orwell against attacks from both communists and right wing cold warriors. When he quotes Orwell as saying that his time as a police officer in Burma was the only time he felt important enough to be hated by large numbers of people, there must be a quiet smile lurking behind the author's text. Both during his lifetime, and even more since, Orwell has been the best kind of stirrer, touching a great many sore points, to the general good, and raising clouds of antagonism in all directions. Not much has changed since Raymond Williams was felt, by one reviewer of his 1971 study of Orwell, to be drawing on asbestos gloves as he began his discussion of Orwell and Spain. Newsinger is effectively vigorous in a manner of which Orwell would have approved in knocking special pleading for the oppressions and deceptions of the Soviet Government under Stalin. He is also perceptive on the tension which Orwell himself seems to have experienced between the belief that truth can never be qualified by consideration of partisan advantage, and a pragmatic decision to accept the least bad alternative from his time at the BBC during the Second World War onwards.

The title of the book is precisely accurate. Newsinger is principally interested in Orwell's politics, not in his political thinking. But he also speculates on what Orwell might have made of the contemporary world. And since the contemporary world is making much of Orwell, this is an important matter. When even the gun lobby in the USA can quote *Animal Farm* in its cause, Orwell's legacy needs urgent consideration. His political thinking is, today, more relevant than his politics. Old battles may not necessarily teach new lessons, but there is a lot in contemporary political argument for which Orwell's thinking is highly relevant.

Orwell, with Laski who died within months of him, is one of the twentieth century's socialists who is being brought back as a useful person to argue with. And if the future does lie with the proles, (and Newsinger insists that this is not a despairing judgment), then we need to know who the proles are, what is the nature of their power, and what it is about them that, in Orwell's terms, leads them, like a plant, to seek the light even without being aware of doing so. This of course raises the difficult question of Orwell's patriotic nationalism, which was one of the elements in his thinking which caused such difficulties for Thompson and the New Left. For Orwell's conception of a socialist revolution which would draw on the existing strengths of the working class rather than on any external principles or yet to be achieved higher consciousness, had clear affinities with Thompson's notion of the key to socialist humanism resting in the collective solidarities of the British, or even English, working class. But it possessed, too, the dangerous negative side of communitarian and nationalist politics: the more we define who we are, the more we exclude those who do not fit the increasingly demanding, because increasingly precise, stereotype. All of which makes Orwell at least as important now as he was fifty years ago at the time of his death, and makes this paperback edition most welcome.

Rodney Barker
Department of Government, London School of Economics & Political Science

The spirit of revolutionary communism

Susan Weissman, *Victor Serge: The course is set on hope* (Verso, London, 2001), xvii + 364pp., ISBN 1-85984-987-3, £22 hbk.

The subject of this careful and thorough biography 'lived from 1890 to 1947, took part in three revolutions, spent a decade in captivity, published more than thirty books. He was born into one exile, died in another and was politically active in seven countries. His life was spent in permanent political opposition.'

The one moment when, as Serge saw it, his libertarian and anti-authoritarian values coincided with a successful and authoritative political act was in October 1917. Whilst he retained a loyalty to the principles of freedom central to his early involvement in anarchism, Serge identified the Bolshevik led revolution in Russia as an example of the realisation of his commitments. It was the effective translation of dreams into reality, with the party of Lenin and Trotsky taking up responsibilities in a way which the movements he'd previously been part of had proved 'incapable of doing'.

By early 1919, after an early career involving years in prison for involvement with a group of violent Belgian and French anarchists, and participation in the failed syndicalist uprising in Barcelona in 1917, Serge had made his way to Petrograd to put himself 'at the service of the revolution. He served on the first staff of the Communist International, showing an industrious and practical commitment to the cause, and fighting in the civil war in defence of his adopted city. Serge remained loyal to the spirit of revolutionary communism throughout the rest of his life—though he would come to the view that the particular institutions and organisations through which the Bolsheviks had applied and projected their politics would never be relevant again.

This insight was the bitter fruit of successive steps of marginalisation and defeat. From his ealiest days in Russia, Serge saw the Bolsheviks' success in achieving revolution as the product of the party's interaction with powerful, radical and democratic currents in society. He celebrated the determination and single-mindedness of those who established Soviet power. But it is now clear from his writings that Serge was, at the least, uneasy about what he saw as unnecessary bureaucratisation in the young state, expressed in a thousand expressions of self-importance and casual arbitrariness on the part of officials.

As Stalin pursued his path to power, a process linked to the changing social composition and bureaucratisation of the Communist Party, Serge returned from his CI posting in Vienna to become active in the opposition movements led by 'old Bolsheviks'. These criticised the party's departures from the culture and traditions it had established for itself and developed independent policy proposals. Following the final defeat of the Trotskyist opposition, Serge again faced years of imprisonment and internal exile. It was during this period that he applied his impressive literary abilities to writing his novels, and chronicling the remarkable and painful experience of the cadre and activists being set up for isolation, persecution and murder.

In many ways, Serge's most significant work followed his flight from the Soviet Union, coming after a campaign by supporters who had seen a rare opportunity to induce Stalin to spare a convicted oppositionist. Apart from continued work on novels which conveyed the atmosphere and intolerable pressures experienced by victims of the terror, Serge now redeveloped his relationship with Trotsky—through correspondence—and so clarified his own political positions.

Serge worked and wrote in line with a 'double duty' he had set himself. This involved defending the achievements of the revolution from those who would attack them. But it also meant not hesitating to criticise the errors and problems in the revolutionary movement resulting from its own failings. Serge came to apply this principle to the opposition movement of which he himself was a part. He raised concerns about the tactics and culture of the groupings which Trotsky led and influenced, arguing that they should develop a less sectarian relationship to other left wing but anti-Stalinist forces.

Following a dispute over the way Trotsky's followers should have operated during the Spanish civil war, an argumentative exchange of correspondence and articles re-evaluating the suppression of a protest by sailors in 1921 in the port of Kronstadt crystallised the differences between Serge and Trotsky. Serge saw that Trotskyism was adopting and promoting a dogmatic, intolerant 'outlook in harmony with the very Stalinism against which it had taken its stand'. His distinctive role within revolutionary communism was to insist on the validity of the project, whilst recognising that it had come to embody itself in self-defeating and unattractive forms.

Weissman is clearly deeply concerned to assert Serge's significance—she has made it a central part of her life's work to produce this layered and respectful account of his life, including material on his family and personal relationships. The empathic tone she achieves is informed by the close collaboration she has enjoyed with Serge's son, Vlady, which helped her contact others who had known the man. Her style is to stay close to Serge, to give a detailed account of his movements, and to describe events as he would have seen and interpreted them. Her accounts of the debates within the opposition movements sometimes read as if she imagines Serge's views on particular questions will be directly useful to those seeking to develop far-left politics now and in the future. Whether or not this is the case, Weissman gives a convincing sense of the temper and the milieu of the movements Serge was part of and summarises and explains many of the discussions which exercised the non-Stalinist left in the 1920s and 1930s.

Victor Serge: The course is set on hope is a substantial intellectual biography. If it lacks one significant thing, this is a sustained critical consideration of Serge's fiction as art. Passages from the novels are excerpted simply to illustrate political points. In spite of this, this book is unlikely to be superseded as the key source of information on and insight into the life and motivations of one of the twentieth century's authentic revolutionaries.

Mike Waite is a member of the editorial board for Socialist History

A courageous woman

Vida Henning, *Woman in a Shabby Brown Coat* (Green Cottage, Bedhampton, 2000), 203pp., ISBN 0-95369-370-8, £7.99 pbk.

This is a heart warming and moving book, a tribute to a rank-and-file woman communist from her daughter. The author describes it as 'The biography of an extraordinary woman', and it is. The left, socialist and communist movement made extraordinary women—and men—out of ordinary ones. It made vocal and passionately articulate people out of those who were supposed to let others, 'the experts', decide important issues; peace or war, poverty or progress.

The intriguing title of this book is taken from a sneering reference to the 'shabby brown-coated woman', Ellen May Cose, whose life the book describes. The sneer was from a local paper in Brighton where she was the communist candidate in a local election. Presumably the paper's readers were expected to think that wearing a mink coat was a guarantee of political acumen and integrity! Ellen's photograph is on the cover. It shows a dignified and beautiful woman of character and determination, and the text shows that she was all these things.

She was born in 1907 and died in 1974. Not a long life, but as we read we see it was a rich and unselfish one, devoted to her family and, by natural extension of feeling, the cause of peace against war, equality against discrimination, the good life for all not the division between privilege and poverty.

An important aspect of the book is its skilled combination of the personal and the political. To realise her potential Ellen had to combat not only the sneers of anti-communist editors but the attitudes of members of the CP including, sadly, her own husband. He had joined the party before his wife and saw her as 'second best', an attitude often met with in the first half of the twentieth century and still encountered in the communist and other left organisations. Ellen also had to suffer physical violence from him and so did their five children.

Ellen's husband wasn't too happy when his party branch urged him, in the mid-1930s, to 'sign up' his wife. Vida writes: 'There was no way he would do this. He knew of her qualities but because of his insecure childhood would not fully recognise that in some respects she was his superior. In fact all their married life he would try to improve his own self-esteem by belittling Ellen.' And, 'he would at times physically batter her in order to prove to himself that he was in charge—he was the stronger' (p.58). But within a short time of arriving in Brighton Ellen was elected to the party district committee. Her husband Harold grumbled about the disruption of his Sunday dinner but it never occurred to him to cook it!

But this chauvinist attitude doesn't lead Vida to dismiss her father completely, despite his bullying. She mentions his hard work and his skills as a decorator and conscientious craftsman. She makes it clear however that he had many serious weaknesses and shortcomings as a husband and a father. These were enough to make his children anti-communist. Yet the author, who understands her parents' views and beliefs, knowing them to be based on a deep love of justice and a determination to help the underdog (especially in Ellen's case), doesn't fall into this trap. A particularly good example of Vida supporting her mother's views is where she quotes letters written by them both and published in the *Morning Star*, on the hoary question of 'women's work' (pp.140–1).

Vida's account of her mother's life and struggles, domestic and political, remind the reader of the way Harry Pollitt wrote about his mother. And how his political views were very much shaped by his hatred for the system which gave her such a small reward for all her hard work.

Yet the picture painted of Ellen—a devoted and hard-working communist who spent her life and energies in political work—doesn't mean that Vida agreed with every facet of party policies. In the late 1960s she and her husband Roy went to Hungary to teach for a year. Vida writes: 'Our stay in Hungary led to some political differences between Ellen and ourselves.' (p.148) And then, talking of Hungarian students they met, she writes: 'But they seemed to be very inhibited about discussing anything even remotely political or critical of the régime. As time went on it became apparent that Hungary was controlled by bureaucrats and politicians who slavishly followed the Soviet line.'

The later years of Ellen's life saw her enjoy some relaxation. She travelled to Australia to see her eldest daughter and, in the course of her return journey, spent short periods in Japan and the USSR.

Vida's love for her unselfish and caring mother shines and glows throughout the book. Even the bullying that Vida suffered at school because her mother was an outspoken communist didn't cause her to resent or repudiate the person or the ideas. The final pages with the description of Ellen's funeral service and then Vida placing on the fence at Greenham Common a precious photograph of her mother are both very moving and beautiful. A proud and graceful tribute to a strong and courageous communist and mother. In the message with the photo Vida wrote: 'I salute Ellen's life and vow that I shall not falter in the struggle to rid humanity from the threat of nuclear holocaust.'

Socialists could produce hundreds of accounts of such self-sacrifice as that displayed by Ellen. Vida Henning's book is fine example to learn from. It weaves the personal with the political in a simple, deft and moving way. An enriching book which could, and should, stimulate the writing of many more accounts of the lives of rank-and-file workers for a better world.

Laurie Green is a member of the Socialist History Society

Mexican havens

Diana Anhalt, *A Gathering of Fugitives. American political expatriates in Mexico 1948–1965* (Archer Books, Santa Maria, 2001), 246pp., ISBN 1-93112-203-2, US$15.00 pbk.

One of the side-effects of McCarthyism in the USA was a minor diaspora of American Communists and others closely associated with the party from the late 1940s who fled to Canada, Central and South America, Western Europe (Paris in particular) and the Soviet bloc countries.[1] British cultural life benefited from several blacklisted actors and film workers (the most significant being the film director Joseph Losey) while the British CP gained at least two experienced party organisers and the *Daily Worker* at least one journalist. Those who left the States did so for a variety of reasons, some because they simply could no longer work in their professional field, others fled abroad to escape arrest or avoid being subpoenaed to appear before the House of Un-American Activities or the various state equivalents. Many CP members had perjured themselves by signing loyalty oaths, declaring that they were not or never had been members of the Communist Party, in order to get jobs in government and even some private businesses, and many were frightened of being found out. Such a loyalty programme was first introduced in Federal employment by Truman in March 1947, nine days after the presentation of the Truman Doctrine and pre-dating McCarthy's rise to prominence. There was a feeling among many CPUSA members that political repression would only get worse and that the United States was on the road to fascism. William Z. Foster believed that war was inevitable between America and the Soviet Union and secret plans were already made in 1947 for the party to go underground. The fear of a fascist future seems to have been the main motivating factor behind the decision of the author's parents to flee to Mexico. It should also be mentioned that a small number of 'undesirable aliens' were also deported at this time from America.

Naturally sanctuary was sought in those countries bordering the USA,

Mexico and Canada, not only because physically they were nearest but also because entry requirements didn't always necessitate a passport. After 1947 it became common practice for the State Department to withhold passports from those considered to be politically suspect, something enshrined in law by the 1950 McCarran Act (a Supreme Court ruling in 1958 eventually curtailed the denial of travel documents as a political weapon). Canada in the early postwar years was not particularly accommodating to leftwing exiles as a result of the well-known 'atomic spy case' in 1946. Mexico, however, had a long tradition of accepting political refugees— 20,000–25,000 Republican exiles from Spain fled to Mexico and Argentina at the end of the Civil War, while of course (ironically enough) Trotsky was allowed to settle down in Mexico City—and a revolutionary 'anti-Yankee' history.[2] It became the predominant place of sanctuary for American political expatriates.

The book under review is an account by the daughter of a married couple of party members who fled in the period of McCarthyism to Mexico, the country which came to have the largest concentration of US political exiles. In many ways the work is motivated by very personal reasons, an attempt to come to grips with her young life being turned upside-down by events of the time. Her parents, Eastern European Jews living in the Bronx and active local communists from the 1930s, suddenly took the decision to leave for Mexico at the end of 1950. They had two girls and the older, the author, was 10 years old at the time and did not find out that they were leaving America for Mexico before she was asked by a fellow passenger on the plane where she was going and found out the destination was not California as she had been told. She was resentful at being dragged from her home, toys, school and friends without the opportunity of exchanging farewells and at being put down in another country and required to learn a new language. As she writes: 'I must have asked my parents why we left the States. They never told me or, if they did, I don't remember their answers but, at some level I knew, just as I knew it was better not to probe.' (p.13) By the time she had decided to find out the reasons for her parents' actions, both of them had passed away. Thus began over a decade of investigation and research that eventually resulted in the publication of this book. Friends of her parents and fellow-expatriates and their children were interviewed (there are 46 interviewees in all) and corresponded with and there has been copious use of FBI files (those the author has managed to procure dealing with her family, but also those dealing with a few of the other 'exiles in Mexico'). The end result is much more than a 'family history'; it is an account of the American political expatriate community in Mexico and is therefore an important contribution to the history of a neglected aspect of McCarthyism. It is written not in an academic style but in an engaging style with descriptions of her searches, the people she meets and her feelings. There are, though, copious footnotes indicating where cited information has been garnered, an extensive bibliography and an appendix with an 'identification of subjects' named in each chapter.

All in all in the course of her research Diana Anhalt identified over 60 families who went to live in Mexico to escape McCarthyism in the United States—in addition a number of others were only temporary residents, some using the country as a transit point to travel on to Western Europe or the Eastern bloc. Those who set up home in Mexico were given the collective term of ACGM—an acronym for the American Communist Group in Mexico—by the FBI who set up an office in Mexico City in order to keep such 'dangerous undesirable' people under observation. In fact a closer watch was kept on those who went to Mexico than if they had stayed in the USA. The name 'Communist Group' says more about the paranoia of the US State than reality and as was admitted in FBI reports the 'Group' was in effect a loose term to cover an association on a social basis of American marxists in Mexico City, who were never organised under party discipline. By no means were they all party members; some had left at the time of the Non-Aggression Pact or when Browder was replaced as party leader in 1945: 'The only pattern I could find was that they were 'lefties', had departed under similar circumstances during a time when their politics were not tolerated by the general public'(p.38). Naturally many who fled to Mexico met regularly and acted very much like an extended family, giving advice as to how to cope in the new society and with the Mexican authorities and helping one another establish a livelihood. Parties and social gatherings were held, monitored by the FBI, but there was no involvement in Mexican politics, although an interest was taken in American and international politics. There were also those who kept themselves to themselves, in particular if they lived outside of the capital. How the individuals and families fared in their new life also varied a great deal. Some integrated fairly rapidly into the surrounding society, eventually gaining Mexican citizenship and 'disappearing from view. Hollywood blacklistees, described as 'nomads', mostly left after a few years, returning to the States simply because they couldn't earn a living. As Howard Fast, a short-stay expatriate in Mexico, put it: 'our lives are our language'. The more working-class 'lefties' seemed to adapt more effectively to their circumstances and the book describes how several eked out a living and started various small businesses (as with the author's own parents).

Once in Mexico it was no guarantee that the 'Yankee lefties' were once and for all safe. All were aware that as foreigners they could at any time be subject to detention or deportation back to the USA. The FBI was not only allowed with impunity to operate on Mexican soil but they also helped in the creation in 1947 of Mexico's own secret police (DFS). This force carried out its own surveillance operations—calculating at one time that there were some 150 American communists living throughout the country—and co-operated to a varying degree with the FBI. Thus in 1951 Mexican agents seized Gus Hall after less than 24 hours in the country to which he had escaped, jumping bail, to avoid being sent to jail. He, as a one-time general secretary of the CPUSA, had stood trial and ten other leading communists had been found guilty in 1950 under the Smith Act. Hall was immediately forcibly escorted back over the border to the American authorities and an increased prison sentence; three years being added to the five years he had already been sentenced to. However, it was in 1957–8 that the ACGM faced the largest number of arrests and deportations (the Mexican authorities acceding more than likely to demands the FBI had been making for years). This resulted from a combination of renewed pressure from the US government in response to the Sterns' affair, a married couple charged with espionage in the States who managed to slip out of Mexico to Czechoslovakia. Shortly after this major labour unrest broke out and the Mexican government cynically used the presence of American 'communists' to discredit those on strike—'it was all the work of foreign agitators'. Once the unrest was over the pressure was relieved. By the 1960s as the ferocity of anti-communism eased in American society the community of exiles began to drift away. The pollution and growing harshness of modern life in Mexico City has without doubt given further impetus to leave, so that today fewer than ten political expatriates or their spouses have been identified as still living in the country.

A number of expatriates were party members who were ordered by the American CP to go underground and instructed to go to Mexico City. There they were to establish a parallel party leadership that would wait in abeyance ready to come into operation in the event of the Communist Party being declared illegal as an organisation in the States. Unfortunately, this is something still clouded in mystery—someone who was to have spoken about this pulled out of an arranged interview—and it is still unknown how many were involved, whether they were known by the general body of political exiles, how they retained links with the party in the States, what happened to them, etc. Such a strategy would have given substance in the minds of the FBI and others that the ACGM was part of a secret subversive plot under orders from Moscow.[3]

All in all it can be said that the book is an important contribution to detailing a relatively unknown aspect of the Cold War and the way McCarthyism affected individual lives—including children! In the case of the author it is possible to draw comfort from the fact that her attachment to her new homeland, Mexico, is self-evident; she married a Mexican and today lives in Mexico City.

Notes

1. Tony Shaw writes that after the second HUAC investigation of Hollywood in 1951: 'a sizeable minority of those "named" and "friendly" witnesses as part or present Communist Party members emigrated to find work. Mexico received the single largest contingent, followed by Britain and France.' *British Cinema and the Cold War*, p.177.
2. The irony being that the CPUSA greeted the assassination of Trotsky and individual CP members were involved in carrying it out. There is a double irony in that American communists supported the use of the Smith act to imprison Trotskyists during the war, the same legislation under which the CP leadership was indicted in 1948 and subsequently sent to jail.
3. For an account of the 'suicidal tactic' of sending members 'underground' see Ellen Schrecker, 'McCarthyism and the decline of American communism, 1945–1960, in *New Studies in the Politics and Culture of US Communism*.

Steve Parsons has written widely on communist history

Recovering women's history

Griselda Carr, *Pit Women. Coal communities in Northern England in the early twentieth century* (Merlin Press, London, 2001), vi+174pp., ISBN 0-850-36495-7, £12.95 pbk.

Carr's slim volume is a welcome addition to the few works which deal with the cultural and social life of mining. In contrast, there is a wealth of material that has examined the structure of the industry, the history of mining disputes and of economic change in mining. Yet the rich culture of the mining village, which was the bedrock of the industry, is rarely examined. In Carr's work this omission is rectified as industry and culture are drawn together in a detailed description of mining life. Her experience as the wife of a miner, and as someone who lived in a mining village for many years, gives a vividness and sense of authenticity to her account. Her sense of belonging, her knowledge of the community and the people of it, give real life to the text. Indeed, it was the experience of women's activity in the strike that led her to look in detail at the communities in which resistance was forged and the history of those communities.

The book covers the period between 1900 and the eve of nationalisation in 1947. This period marked the pinnacle of the industry, in about 1912, and the subsequent decline of mining in the next decades. In the first part of the book she gives an overview of the industry and the mining communities it generated. These forty pages summarise the history of the industry, the formation of mining communities and the gendered place of women within those communities. With such a large topic to cover, the pace of the early section is somewhat breathless, but also as a result very densely packed and informative. At the least, this summary makes the book a useful introduction to the subject and an indispensable reference point for the newcomer. Yet the real strength of the work is not as an overview, but in the wealth of well-observed detail that Carr crams into the rest of the pages. She provides a rich and detailed slice through life in a pit village during that period. She shows us the appalling conditions in which women had to raise their families. The picture is a disturbingly accurate one of poor sanitation, lack of running water and inadequate heating. Women's domestic lives were blighted by these conditions, where constantly damp clothes and constantly heating water contributed to an unhealthy and dangerous atmosphere for children. Household accidents were common and infant mortality rates in mining communities were the highest in the country. This was a world where women's work was, literally, never done. The woman of the house would rise with the first man to go on shift and would not rest until the last worker had returned from the pit head to be bathed and fed. The introduction of pit head baths removed some of the dirt and danger from the mining home, but that home would not be transformed until the nationalisation of the industry.

Carr also provides fascinating insights into the socialisation of girls in mining communities. Little was expected of young women, and there were few opportunities open to them. The vast majority of young women either followed in their mothers' footsteps or, an even less appealing option, entered domestic service. Girls were trained to work at home from an early age and could sometimes shoulder the domestic burden of caring for fathers and brothers at a young age. In the last part of the book Carr turns to the networks that women forged in the course of their domestic labours and the formal organisations which supported them. The Women's Co-operative Guilds were very popular in mining communities and were linked to the strength of the co-operative movement amongst mining women. At the end of the book she gives us some idea of the impact that major disputes had on women's lives, something which has rarely been examined in any literature.

Pit Women is an undeniably vivid piece of social history. Carr's concern is to make very clear the vital role of women in mining families, and in this she succeeds. These were families that historically operated as collective productive units. Her account illuminates the way in which all members of the unit worked for the good of the whole. The mining industry could not have survived without women's work to ensure a clean, fed and healthy work force, managed on a shoestring budget.

Yet despite this emphasis, it is not a book which focuses exclusively on women, or which interrogates gender relations. There is a tendency for the women to appear as passive, stalwart domestic organisers, dedicated to husband and children. Carr's attention to the drudgery of domestic life tends to outweigh her later chapters in which we have more of a sense of the women as actors. Even when she details the organisation of women during the 1926 lockout, mining women do not appear as resourceful players. The reality was that women were active in 1926. Many miners' wives were involved in collecting, picketing and speaking during the lockout. A group of wives toured Russia, speaking and collecting for mining communities in 1926. These women were not the leaders of the movement, but they were central to the grassroots work of Marion Phillips's Women's Committee for the Relief of Miners Wives and Children.

This absence and passivity at times lets the book down. Women's activity was a minority experience, and as such has been written out of history. Yet it is this very activity which was the precursor to the blossoming of women's groups in the 1984/5 strike. Even the title of the last chapter implies that women were the victims rather than the protagonists in disputes in the early part of the century—'The Impact of some Prolonged Industrial Struggles on Women's Lives'. Despite this, the book remains an invaluable resource. Richly detailed, thoroughly researched and well written, it is an invaluable addition to work that chronicles social life in mining communities.

Meg Allen recently completed a PhD at the University of Manchester on women in the 1984/85 miners' strike

A love–hate relationship

Paul Allender, *What's Wrong with Labour? A critical history of the Labour Party in the twentieth century* (Merlin Press, London, 2001), xii+176pp., ISBN 0-85036-497-3, £12.95 pbk.

The question of what we should think of the Labour Party is not new. It is the party which socialists love to hate, yet as a friend commented the day I wrote this review, 'there isn't anything else'. Of course that is wrong and of course there are lots of 'other' parties, but most of us became socialists because we could see a grossly unfair world which we wanted to change. And we could see also that if that was to be done, from the British perspective there was only one possible vehicle.

There is a whole industry involved in analysing the Labour Party and spelling out its blemishes in detail. Perhaps the industry began with Ralph Miliband's influential Parliamentary Socialism, a book first published in 1961 but which Paul Allender implies dates from 1972, an error not without importance (even then, what of earlier critics like R.H. Tawney and Harold Laski?). It is one of the virtues of Allender's book that he spends a good deal of space defining labourism, a term which he attributes as a concept to Miliband, and that he explores the concept probably more fully than any predecessor. Perhaps the best brief definition he gives is: 'lack of ideology, vagueness, contradiction and defeatism' (p.155). Elsewhere, he points to a hazy commitment to an undefined social justice, class collaborationism, trade unionism masquerading as the national interest and concentration on electoralism, though it is perhaps questionable whether this latter is a proper criticism of a political party.

It is tolerably clear after a century that the Labour Party is not and has never been a socialist party and that its grasp of ideology is weak. Most people would agree in general terms with Allender, though some Labour Party members (he left the party in 1985) would put the qualities which he discerns in a more complimentary light. The power of the party leader, rightly stressed in the book, is now probably greater than ever before. Allender points out that leader after leader has betrayed the principles of the party, such as they were, and that the term social justice has always been a vague concept capable of accommodating a multitude of definitions. This is presumably why Tony Blair has been able to shift the party from what was thought to be the political left to what Blair rightly describes as the centre with little outcry from within its ranks. It is one of the book's virtues that it shows that the Labour Party has not basically changed its spots and that what has latterly been called 'new Labour' is more important for its similarities with the past than its differences.

The real question after the century is not what Labour stands for but why; and here Allender, like Miliband before him, is not much help. An explanation is obviously beyond the scope of a review but it would be nice to see a book which acknowledges that political parties and their leaders are creatures of their time and culture and have little or no independent life. A world of mass poverty and mass trade unionism produced leaders like MacDonald and Attlee (the radicalism of the latter exaggerated by the anti-fascism of the 1930s and the leftward tendencies of the war years), while the breakup of heavy industry, the decline of the importance of social class, the coming of feminism and mass migration produced a Blair. It is not much more complicated than that, but one would have hoped to find a substantial chapter devoted to the subject. Again, the lack of socialism amongst the British people as a whole deserves some analysis and explanation. It would be perfectly fair for the Labour leaders to say that if there had been a mass demand for socialism Britain would now be a socialist country. Betrayal by the leadership is an easy charge but it is really not good enough.

The book consists of four chapters of which only one, of some thirty pages, is a proper 'short history of the British Labour Party'. The first and last chapters are devoted to the author's analysis of labourism, and the only other chapter is a study of Labour in Sheffield, the author's birthplace, between 1973 and 1988. This is of much interest, but it sometimes sits uneasily with the remainder of the book. How Sheffield deindustrialised in these years, losing nearly 100,000 jobs (its region lost 173,000) in 1978–98, and becoming in the end a leading telephone call centre, is documented in detail, but again one cannot but feel that the author's local knowledge and hard work (including a number of taped interviews) deserve expression at greater length. The connection between the local and the national scene is made on p.121 (and, to be fair, in a few other places), where the author concludes that the labour movement in Sheffield lacked the 'ideas and arguments' with which to defend the working class against the tide of unemployment which faced it: 'It was part of a tradition that had spurned theory and ideology over eighty years earlier and thus was left with nowhere to turn but to local capitalists who were loyal to Sheffield.'

David Rubinstein
Hon. Fellow, University of York

A publishing and educational phenomenon

Paul Laity (ed.), *Left Book Club Anthology* (Gollancz, London, 2001), xxxi+254pp., ISBN 0-575-07221-0, £20 hbk.

The Left Book Club was a publishing success story, publishing 260 titles and selling millions of books in its thirteen-year life. It was an educational success story, with 40,000 members by the end of the first year; by 1939 it had a membership of 57,000. And it was a political success story, helping to shape informed public opinion for a generation (Attlee's 1945 government included eight LBC authors).

All this is justly celebrated and remembered in this sixtieth anniversary anthology, ably edited and introduced by Paul Laity. Although it includes extracts from only thirteen LBC choices published between 1936 and 1941, they range pretty well across the club's interests. There is eye-witness documentary (Edgar Snow's *Red Star Over China*, Arthur Koestler's *Spanish Testament*, G.E.R. Gedeye's *Fallen Bastions*), drama (*Waiting for Lefty*), autobiography (B.L. Coombes's *These Poor Hands*, Wilf Macartney's *Walls Have Mouths*), song (from the Swingler-Bush *Left Song Book*), science (H.J. Muller's *Out of the Night*), polemic (Orwell's *The Road to Wigan Pier*, Stephen Spender's *Forward from Liberalism*, Gollancz's own *The Betrayal of the Left*), fiction (Jan Petersen's *Our Street*) and the club 'bible', John Strachey's *The Theory and Practice of Socialism*. Each is a powerful example of 1930s writing, main-line junctions on that mythical 1930s journey to the border—Parkhurst, New York, Lancashire, Yenan, South Wales, Malaga, Vienna, Berlin, Prague, Hampstead. Particularly vivid are Gedeye's account of Vienna after the Anschluss, the story of Coombes' first shift underground, and Snow's tale of meeting Chou En Lai. And although Laity attributes the text of 'Question and Answer' to Randall Swingler instead of G.R. Atterbury, the inclusion of three songs from the—now extremely rare—*Left Song Book* is to be welcomed.

But the best thing about the book is Laity's lively introduction, which discusses some of the sources of the club's success (conventionally explained by reference to the personality of Gollancz or the 'intensity' of the period), the sociology of its members, the nature of its contribution to the intellectual culture of the 1930s and 1940s (in particular the publication of so many eye-witness documentaries) and its long-term educational contribution (via the ABCA) to the postwar consensus. Drawing on *Left News*, Laity offers a fascinating and well-researched account of this extraordinary organisation, its leaders, its members, its successes and failures as well as some of its endearing idiosyncrasies.

As with any anthology, there are bound to be arguments about Laity's selection. Arguably too much space is given to Orwell, Spender and Koestler, writers whose work is not difficult to find, whose relationship with the club was brief, to say the least, and who are best-known today because they subsequently repudiated everything the club tried to achieve. The selection also gives the impression that the LBC effectively ended in the autumn of 1939, when almost half the club's books were published after that date (including Wal Hannington's *Lean Years*, Murray Constantine's *Swastika Night*, Margot Heinemann's *Britain's Coal* and Max Cohen's *I Was One of the Unemployed*). And though it is not difficult to see why Laity does not include any of the club's more gruesome accounts of Actually Existing Socialism in the book, they nevertheless represented an important aspect of the club's agenda and of the thinking of its members.

Moreover, as the reception of this book demonstrated, interest in the LBC remains curiously preoccupied by what the *New Statesman* called the club's 'knee-trembling weakness for Stalin'. For the *Guardian* this is an anthology of 'the original loony left', 'a compressed statement in the long history of English naivety', 'violently pro-Stalin, anti-fascist, bien-pensant', 'naïve at best, deplorable at worst'. For Valentine Cunningham in the *London Review of Books*, even the location of the club's offices is grounds for suspicion—'naturally, the club was a front for the Communist Party of Great Britain, for Moscow's men and women in Covent Garden's King Street—conveniently just around the corner from the Gollancz offices in Henrietta Street…'

The idea that the LBC is a monument to the folly of the British left in the 1930s, and the perfidy of the Communist Party in particular, has long been a commonplace in Cold War history. For Henry Pelling the LBC was a 'Communist "satellite" organisation'; Neal Wood wrote darkly about 'communist penetration' of the LBC. More recently, Stephen Koch, in *Double Lives: Stalin, Willi Munzenberg and the Seduction of the Intellectuals* (1995) has argued that the LBC was the 'point of intersection between propaganda and espionage'. Apparently funded by Otto Katz to 'promote Stalinist chic' on behalf of the Soviet *apparat*, the LBC was one of the crucial ways in which 'Stalinist opinion was "networked" in England'. For Koch, the 'Communist conspiracy in Britain' operated on two levels, connected by 'the language of the democratic elites and the language of revolt':

> On the public level, the move to Stalinize Bloomsbury taste was led by Otto Katz and the Munzenberg apparatus, using British fronts such as the Left Book Club and its many appendages. Covertly, the process was led by Blunt and his gofer, Burgess, guided by Maly and by Ludwik's Recruit in the London offices of the Secret Intelligence Services (SIS), silently sustained by the talent-spotters throughout the universities and in the Munzenberg-Gilbarti propaganda network, and tied to the Soviets through a dual NKVD-Comintern network running through Amsterdam, Berlin and Paris. (p.5)

This is all richly suggestive in the best Cold War manner. Koch's assertion that Otto Katz wrote several LBC titles under pseudonym is credited to an unnamed source in British Intelligence. Wood's evidence of CP 'penetration' of the club is the fact that one in six members were also CP members (would it have been less of a conspiracy if fewer CP members had joined the LBC?) Pelling's proof that the club 'served the ends of the Communist Party' is that a book by August Thalheimer was once rejected by the club's selection committee.

But it is difficult to know if any of this amounts to a 'conspiracy'. The LBC was quite open about its intention to influence educated opinion. No one was ever forced to join the LBC. No members can have been under any illusion about the club's politics when they joined. If they did not like the club's Monthly Choices, they did not have to read them. Less than half of the books in the years 1936–40 were written by CP members. Only twelve titles before 1939 dealt with conditions in the Soviet Union. Anyway, why was the LBC so successful when the Labour Party Book Club and the Right Book Club were such risible failures?

The answer surely lies less in the personalities and politics of the selection committee than in the activities of LBC members and groups. By 1939 there were 1,200 local and specialist LBC discussion groups, including groups for London taxi drivers, architects, teachers, railwaymen, lawyers, accountants, poets, cyclists, musicians, puppeteers, scientists, postmen and sixth-formers. A greater understanding of what these groups did on the ground ought at least to clarify the nature of the 'conspiracy'.

For example, in May 1938 the LBC Writers and Readers Group (which was supported by Stephen Spender, Christopher Isherwood and Rebecca West), together with the LBC Musicians, Actors, and Amateur Theatre Groups, organised a Left Book Club 'Theatre Festival and Cultural Week'. The festival included a performance at the Scala Theatre of a new version (by Randall Swingler and Alan Bush) of Handel's oratorio Belshazzar (sponsored by the London Co-operative Societies Joint Education Committee), an exhibition organised by the LBC Scientists Group, a lecture-recital by the LBC Poetry Group of 'Declamatory Poetry Throughout the Ages', a debate organised by the Artists International Association and a Music-Drama festival under the auspices of the WMA and the LBC Theatre Guild (judged by Miles Malleson, Andre van Gyseghem, Parry Jones, John Ireland and Edward Clark). The week ended with a debate at the Conway Hall on 'Literature and the People' between Elmer Rice, Norman Collins, AE Coppard, Richard Church, Daniel George, Richard Goodman, John Strachey, Olaf Stapledon, Rose Macaulay, LAG Strong and Rex Warner.

Otto Katz and the NKVD must have despaired when they saw how all those roubles were being spent. If this was the LBC in action, it made for a pretty extraordinary conspiracy. But then, as this brave and splendid anthology reminds us, the Left Book Club was a pretty extraordinary phenomenon.

Andy Croft is a freelance writer and poet living in Middlesborough

Socialist History Journal

The *Socialist History Journal* explores and assesses the past of the socialist movement and broader processes in relation to it, not only for the sake of historical understanding, but as an input and contribution to the movement's future development. The journal is not exclusive and welcomes argument and debate from all viewpoints.

Other *Socialist History* titles

A Bourgeois Revolution?
Socialist History 1 · 1993
0 7453 0805 8

What Was Communism? Pt 1
Socialist History 2 · 1993
0 7453 0806 6

What Was Communism? Pt 2
Socialist History 3 · 1993
0 7453 08074 1

The Labour Party Since 1945
Socialist History 4 · 1994
0 7453 0808 2

The Left and Culture
Socialist History 5 · 1994
0 7453 0809 0

The Personal and the Political
Socialist History 6 · 1994
0 7453 0810 4

Fighting the Good Fight?
Socialist History 7 · 1995
0 7453 1061 3

Historiography and the British Marxist Historians
Socialist History 8 · 1995
0 7453 0812 0

Labour Movements
Socialist History 9 · 1996
0 7453 0813 9

Revisions?
Socialist History 10 · 1996
0 7453 0814 7

The Cold War
Socialist History 11 · 1997
0 7453 1241 1

Nationalism and Communist Party History
Socialist History 12 · 1997
0 7453 1267 5

Imperialism and Internationalism
Socialist History 13 · 1998
1 85489 107 3

The Future of History
Socialist History 14 · 1998
1 85489 109 X

Visions of the Future
Socialist History 15 · 1999
1 85489 115 4

America and the Left
Socialist History 16 · 1999
1 85489 117 0

International and Comparative Labour History
Socialist History 17 · 2000
1 85489 119 7

Cultures and Politics
Socialist History 18 · 2000
1 85489 123 5

Life Histories
Socialist History 19 · 2001
1 85489 129 4

Contested Legacies
Socialist History 20 · 2001
1 85489 135 9

Red Lives
Socialist History 21 · 2002
1 85489 141 3